From Risk Profiling to Enterprise Resilience

From Risk Profiling to Enterprise Resilience introduces readers to a new approach to risk profiling theory and methodology, as well as relationships between an enterprise's risk profile and its resilience to crises.

Given the need to reflect on changes in approaches to risk and risk management in the aftermath of the COVID-19 pandemic, the book attempts to characterize the interdependencies between risk profiling processes and the processes of shaping and improving enterprise resilience. After reading the book, the readers will firstly gain theoretical knowledge of risk management in non-crisis and crisis conditions, risk mitigation and risk profiling. Secondly, they will also acquire the practical skills of performing risk profiling, identifying risk mitigation actions, perceiving relationships between individual enterprises' risk profiles (and their changes), and the building and improving of their resilience. The inclusion of graphics, tables, diagrams, charts, instructions and recommendations will make the content is also easy to understand for a non-specialist audience.

This book will be of great interest entrepreneurs, managers and risk management professionals, who can use the content included in the book in their management processes, as well as stakeholders of various enterprises, business and academic communities and students of all levels.

Sylwia Bąk holds a PhD in Management Sciences. She is Assistant Professor and works as a Researcher and Lecturer in the Management Systems Department of Jagiellonian University in Cracow, Poland.

Piotr Jedynak is Professor of Management. He works at Jagiellonian University in Cracow, Poland, where he holds the positions of University Rector and Head of the Management Systems Department.

Routledge Focus on Business and Management

The fields of business and management have grown exponentially as areas of research and education. This growth presents challenges for readers trying to keep up with the latest important insights. *Routledge Focus on Business and Management* presents small books on big topics and how they intersect with the world of business research.

Individually, each title in the series provides coverage of a key academic topic, whilst collectively, the series forms a comprehensive collection across the business disciplines.

Artificial Intelligence and Project Management
An Integrated Approach to Knowledge-Based Evaluation
Tadeusz A. Grzeszczyk

Organizational Aesthetics
Artful Visual Representations of Business and Organizations
Barbara Fryzel and Aleksander Marcinkowski

Open Strategy for Digital Business
Managing in ICT-Driven Environments
Ewa Lechman, Joanna Radomska and Ewa Stańczyk-Hugiet

Purpose-driven Innovation Leadership for Sustainable Development
A Qualitative Case Study Approach
Gaia Grant

Evolution of the Global Fitness Industry
Strategy, Sustainability and Innovation
Patrizia Gazzola, Enrica Pavione and Francesco Ferrazzano

For more information about this series, please visit: www.routledge.com/Routledge-Focus-on-Business-and-Management/book-series/FBM

From Risk Profiling to Enterprise Resilience

Interdependencies in Management

Sylwia Bąk and Piotr Jedynak

LONDON AND NEW YORK

First published 2024
by Routledge
4 Park Square, Milton Park, Abingdon, Oxon OX14 4RN

and by Routledge
605 Third Avenue, New York, NY 10158

Routledge is an imprint of the Taylor & Francis Group, an informa business

British Library Cataloguing-in-Publication Data
A catalogue record for this book is available from the British Library

ISBN: 978-1-032-84691-0 (hbk)
ISBN: 978-1-032-84694-1 (pbk)
ISBN: 978-1-003-51453-4 (ebk)

DOI: 10.4324/9781003514534

Typeset in Times New Roman
by KnowledgeWorks Global Ltd.

Contents

Preface   *vii*
Introduction   *viii*

1 Enterprise risk management in non-crisis and crisis
   environments   1

   1.1   Standard risk management systems 1
   1.2   Non-standard risk management systems 5
   Bibliography 10

2 Risk mitigation   14

   2.1   Types of mitigation actions 14
   2.2   Risk mitigation actions in crisis situations 16
   Bibliography 19

3 Risk profiling   23

   3.1   The essence of a risk profile 23
   3.2   The structure of a risk profile 25
   3.3   The roles and functions of risk profiling
   *   in business operations 28*
   Bibliography 30

4 Research methodology   31

   4.1   Research objectives and questions 31
   4.2   Data sources 32
   4.3   Research methods 33
   Bibliography 34

5 Impact of the COVID-19 pandemic on the risk
profiles of the selected enterprises representing the
financial, construction and IT sectors 36

5.1 *Impact of the pandemic on the modification
of the risk profiles of the analysed
enterprises – A sectoral approach 36*
5.1.1 *Financial sector 36*
5.1.2 *Construction sector 39*
5.1.3 *IT sector 42*
5.2 *The impact of the pandemic on modifications
to the risk profiles of the analysed
enterprises – An inter-sectoral comparison 45*
Appendices 48

6 Risk mitigation actions employed by the analysed
enterprises representing the financial, construction
and IT sectors implemented during the course of the
COVID-19 pandemic 70

6.1 *Strategic changes 70*
6.2 *Changes in business models 70*
6.3 *Operational changes 71*
6.4 *Digital transformation 72*
6.5 *Changes in market relations 72*
6.6 *Risk management 73*
6.7 *Finance management 73*

7 Risk profiling and enterprise resilience 75

7.1 *The impact of risk management on the
creation of resilience mechanisms 75*
7.2 *The role of risk profiling in measuring
and improving enterprise resilience 77*
7.3 *Practical implications of the interdependencies
between risk profiling and enterprise resilience 79*
Bibliography 81

Conclusions 83

Index 87

Preface

In our opinion, there is a need to reflect on changes in approaches to risk and risk management caused by the COVID-19 pandemic. Therefore, in this book, we attempt to characterize the interdependencies between risk profiling processes and the processes of shaping and improving enterprise resilience. The main objective of the book is to introduce readers to a new approach to risk profiling theory and methodology, as well as relationships between an enterprise's risk profile and its resilience to crises. After reading the book, the potential reader will firstly gain theoretical knowledge of risk management in non-crisis and crisis conditions, risk mitigation and risk profiling. Secondly, they should also acquire the practical skills of performing risk profiling, identifying risk mitigation actions and perceiving relationships between individual enterprises' risk profiles (and their changes) and the building and improving of their resilience. Due to the format of this book, which uses various graphic forms, tables, diagrams, charts, instructions, recommendations, etc., the content is also easily assimilable for a non-specialist audience. In summary, this book aims to update and integrate the knowledge of risk management (particularly at the risk profiling stage) and enterprise resilience in the current business environment, determined by the changes resulting from the course of the COVID-19 pandemic. The book is therefore addressed to entrepreneurs, managers and risk management professionals, who can use the model and other information included in the book in their management processes, as well as stakeholders of various enterprises, the business and academic communities and students of all levels.

Sylwia Bąk and Piotr Jedynak

Credits

The publication has been supported by a grant from the Faculty of Management and Social Communication under the Strategic Programme Excellence Initiative at the Jagiellonian University.

Introduction

The COVID-19 pandemic not only changed the business environment of companies, but also deeply penetrated their core processes, strategies and performance (Jedynak & Bąk, 2021; Li et al., 2021). The accumulation of phenomena accompanying the pandemic and exerting influence on enterprises (regardless of the sector represented) resulted in a number of new and surprising challenges for managers, which forced them to intensify activities in the areas of risk management or crisis management (Kaushal & Srivastava, 2021). Indeed, the COVID-19 pandemic was very quickly labelled a crisis directly affecting companies and the business sphere (Cepel et al., 2020; Fabeil et al., 2020; Galindo-Martín et al., 2021; Hossain et al., 2022; Zadeh, 2022).

The varying situation of the different sectors of the economy meant that companies were affected to varying degrees by the negative consequences of the situation, and sometimes even experienced positive changes associated with it. Thus, some organizations faced the challenges of negative aspects of risks, while others exploited opportunities provided by positive risks. Coping with the pandemic situation, companies focused, firstly, on mitigating risks and combating their own weaknesses and, secondly, on exploiting emerging opportunities and developing their strengths (Jedynak & Bąk, 2021).

During the course of the pandemic, the exposure of companies to various risks induced marked changes in the maturity level of their risk management systems (Bąk & Jedynak, 2023), mainly due to the multiplicity of new challenges (Saragih et al., 2021) and the overestimation of the effectiveness and unreliability of existing defence mechanisms (Engelhardt & White, 2021; Wilke, 2020). The results of these pandemic-induced changes included modifications in risk management culture (Dawson, 2020; Jivaasha, 2021), modifications in organizational structures responsible for risk (Koekemoer et al., 2021) and modifications in risk management (Basak & Zhou, 2020).

In terms of risk management, the most visible changes that took place in enterprises during the pandemic, regardless of the sector represented, were modifications to their risk profiles. There were shifts in exposure to previously identified risks and, above all, a very large number of new risks emerged, which companies only started to experience during the pandemic. Such new risks often appeared abruptly, which made them troublesome to manage because of their unpredictability and enterprises' complete unpreparedness for their occurrence. Problems with managing these risks revealed very strong inadequacies of the resilience mechanisms that companies had developed prior to the pandemic, but which simply did not work in the pandemic crisis situation. It was therefore necessary to update the existing systems for risk management, crisis management and eventually the system for building and strengthening resilience.

The purpose of chapter one is to compare risk management processes applied in non-crisis and crisis settings. In this chapter, we review the similarities and differences between standard and non-standard risk management systems used in business organizations. We pay particular attention to the evolution of crisis management systems, looking in detail at the impact of crises on risk and risk management. We also show precisely how changes in risk management systems implemented during crises trigger the transformation of standard systems to their non-standard or unconventional versions. For this purpose, we use the case of the COVID-19 pandemic.

The objective of chapter two is to explore risk mitigation actions as determinants of the effectiveness of a risk management system. In this chapter, we present an extended definition and detailed classification of mitigation actions, dividing them into process categories. We also propose a catalogue of mitigation actions that enterprises can use to enhance the effectiveness of their risk management systems and develop resilience mechanisms, in both normal and crisis circumstances of conducting business activities, regardless of sector, company size or other variable exogenous and endogenous factors.

Chapter three aims to present our original theory and methodology for corporate risk profiling. In the first part of this chapter, we conceptualize and extend the definition of risk profile and discuss in detail its role in business management. This is followed by a presentation of the risk profile framework structure and the proposed methodology for designing a step-by-step procedure for building, updating and managing a risk profile. In the final section of this chapter, we describe the roles and functions of the risk profiling process in business activities. We put forward arguments for the need for risk profiling in both non-crisis and crisis situations.

The goal of chapter four is to present the methodology of the conducted empirical research. In this chapter, we set out our research objectives and questions, define the stages of the conducted research process, develop a catalogue of the methods and tools used in the research process and describe the data sources used in the research process. The main objective of our research was to identify the risk profiles of selected companies representing the financial, construction and IT sectors before and during the COVID-19 pandemic. We also set five specific objectives. For the research, we qualified 107 companies from the financial (28), construction (38) and IT (41) sectors, all of them listed on the Warsaw Stock Exchange both before and still during the pandemic.

The purpose of chapter five is to present the first part of the results of our empirical research. In this chapter, we describe the risk profiles of the analysed enterprises on a sectoral basis, both before and during the pandemic. In this way, we identify the modifications that the pandemic crisis (in each sector separately) caused in the risk profiles of the selected companies representing the financial, construction and IT sectors. In the next section of this chapter, we show the impact of the pandemic on modifying the risk profiles of the analysed companies, but on a cross-sectoral basis. This allowed us to compare the respective sectors' exposure to individual risk factors during the pandemic.

The purpose of chapter six is to present the second portion of the results of our empirical research. In this chapter, we present the identified and originally categorized risk mitigation actions employed in the analysed enterprises of the financial, construction and IT sectors during the pandemic. We looked for such actions in the internal documentation of the respective companies. The quoted fragments of the indicated source documents underwent a qualitative content analysis and were coded accordingly. The results of this analysis form the final part of the chapter. On this basis, we were able to develop a visualization reflecting the classification and comparison of the mitigation actions implemented during the pandemic.

The goal of chapter seven is to identify the relationships and interdependencies between risk profiling processes and the processes of building and improving enterprise resilience, based on the theoretical considerations presented in the previous chapters and the results of the conducted empirical research. In the first part of this chapter, we analyse the impact of risk management on creating resilience mechanisms in business organizations. In the second part, we detail the relations of risk profiling to enterprise resilience, highlighting the role of profiling in the processes of measuring and improving resilience. In the final section of the chapter, we present practical implications of our empirical research.

Bibliography

Bąk, S., Jedynak, P. (2023). Risk Management Maturity: A Multidimensional Model. London, New York: Routledge. DOI: 10.4324/9781003330905

Basak, B. D., Zhou, Z. (2020). Diffusing Coordination Risk. American Economic Review, 110(1), 271–297. DOI: 10.1257/aer.20171034

Cepel, M., Gavurova, B., Dvorsky, J., Belas, J. (2020). The Impact of the COVID-19 Crisis on the Perception of Business Risk in the SME Segment. Journal Of International Studies, 13(3), 248–263. DOI: 10.14254/2071-8330.2020/13-3/16

Dawson, I. G. J. (2020). Taking Responsibility: Self- Attribution for Risk Creation and Its Influence on the Motivation to Engage in Risk Management Behaviours. Journal of Risk Research, 23(11), 1440–1451. DOI: 10.1080/13669877.2019.1673802

Engelhardt, L., White, A. (2021). Pandemic Response: Risk Planning in Times of a Crisis United International Business Schools in Amsterdam. American Journal of Management, 21(4), 16–30. https://pesquisa.bvsalud.org/global-literature-on-novel-coronavirus-2019-ncov/resource/pt/covidwho-1414296 (Access: 12.04.2023).

Fabeil, N., Pazim, K., Langgat, J. (2020). The Impact of Covid-19 Pandemic Crisis on Micro-Enterprises: Entrepreneurs' Perspective on Business Continuity and Recovery Strategy. Journal of Economics and Business, 3(2), 1–9. DOI: 10.31014/aior.1992.03.02.241

Galindo-Martín, M., Castaño-Martínez, M., Méndez-Picazo, M. (2021). Effects of the Pandemic Crisis on Entrepreneurship and Sustainable Development. Journal of Business Research, 137, 345–353. DOI: 10.1016/j.jbusres.2021.08.053

Hossain, M., Akhter, F., Sultana, M. (2022). SMEs in Covid-19 Crisis and Combating Strategies: A Systematic Literature Review (SLR) and A Case from Emerging Economy. Operations Research Perspectives, 9, 100222. DOI: 10.1016/j.orp.2022.100222

Jedynak, P., Bąk, S. (2021). Risk Management in Crisis: Winners and Losers During the COVID-19 Pandemic, London, New York: Routledge. DOI: 10.4324/9781003131366

Jivaasha, D. D. (2021). Enterprise Risk Management Culture – the Testament of Effective Corporate Governance. Bimaquest, 21(1), 25–33. http://bimaquest.niapune.org.in/index.php/bimaquest/article/view/89 (Access: 11.04.2023).

Kaushal, V., Srivastava, S. (2021). Hospitality and Tourism Industry Amid COVID-19 Pandemic: Perspectives on Challenges and Learnings from India. International Journal of Hospitality Management, 92, 1–9. DOI: 10.1016/j.ijhm.2020.102707

Koekemoer, L., Beer, L. T. D., Govender, K., Brouwers, M. (2021). Leadership Behaviour, Team Effectiveness, Technological Flexibility, Work Engagement and Performance During COVID- 19 Lockdown: An Exploratory Study. SA Journal of Industrial Psychology, 47, 1–9. DOI: 10.4102/sajip.v47i0.1829

Li, J.-Y., Sun, R., Tao, W., Lee, Y. (2021). Employee Coping With Organizational Change in the Face of a Pandemic: The Role of Transparent Internal Communication. Public Relations Review, 47(1), 101984. DOI: 10.1016/j.pubrev.2020.101984

Saragih, S., Setiawan, S., Markus, T., Rhian, P. (2021). Benefits and Challenges of Telework During The Covid-19 Pandemic. International Journal of Business Studies, 14(2), 129–136. DOI: 10.21632/irjbs.14.2.129-135

Wilke, A. (2020). Canadian Employee Safety Considerations During the COVID-19 Pandemic. Plans & Trusts, 30–32. https://blog.ifebp.org/canadian-employee-safety-covid-19/ (Access: 17.04.2023).

Zadeh, F. G. (2022). Entrepreneurship and SMEs Under COVID-19 Crisis: A Literature Review. International Entrepreneurship Review, 8(3), 23–35. DOI: 10.15678/IER.2022.0803.02

1 Enterprise risk management in non-crisis and crisis environments

1.1 Standard risk management systems

Risk management is a component of a holistic business management system that aims to ensure an enterprise's survival and growth even in unpredictable and volatile environments. Understood in this way, risk management is one of the leading objectives of business organizations (Christopher et al., 2011; Elahi, 2013; Bromiley et al., 2015). The place of risk management in a corporate management system is graphically depicted in Figure 1.1.

A systemic approach to management makes it possible to treat risk management as not only one component of an enterprise management system but also a separate system integrating management domains, hierarchical levels, processes and relationships. Undoubtedly, a risk management system is one of the most important and mandatory systems for effective enterprise management, which activates processes for responding to stimuli coming from the complex business environment (Fischer et al., 2010; Dionne, 2013).

In the standard view, risk management actually functions as a separate system, but one that is strongly integrated with other management dimensions and strategic objectives (Schiller & Prpich, 2012). What follows is that there are many functions that a standard risk management system performs in an enterprise. These functions can be divided based on several criteria (Jedynak & Bąk, 2021), for example:

- an enterprise's strategy:
  - risk management as an enterprise's leading strategic objective,
  - risk management as a determinant of ensuring business continuity,
  - risk management as a factor in corporate success,
  - risk management as a management imperative,
  - risk management as a source of competitive advantage.

- management processes:
  - risk management as one of the processes of strategic management,

DOI: 10.4324/9781003514534-1

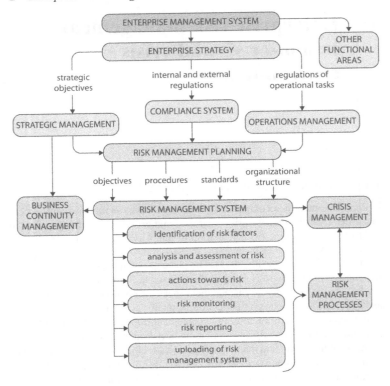

Figure 1.1 The place of risk management in a corporate management system
Source: The authors' own work based on Jedynak and Bąk (2021).

- a business management system:
  - risk management as a separate management system,
  - risk management as a subsystem of business management,
  - risk management as an element of other business management subsystems.
- management domains:
  - risk management as an obligatory element of an enterprise's all management domains and functional areas,
  - risk management as a specialist management domain,
  - risk management as a function of business management.

- managers' competencies:
  - risk management as a managerial specialization,
  - risk management as a determinant of managerial competencies.
- complexity and integration of management systems:
  - risk management as a rationale for integrating management systems,
  - risk management as an integrated management system,
  - risk management as a response to the complexity of management systems.
- management concepts:
  - risk management as an obligatory element of management concepts.

The most popular and standard form of a risk management system is enterprise risk management (ERM). ERM is an approach to risk that, according to one of its earliest definitions, represents a continuous process by which enterprises, regardless of sector, can assess, control, finance and monitor risks from a variety of sources to improve stakeholder value, in both the short and long term (D'Arcy & Brogan, 2001). Another approach to defining ERM indicates that it is a structured and disciplined management approach, which enables managers to understand uncertainty and risk as well as to manage them in an integrated and comprehensive manner (Sobel & Reding, 2004). Thus, in summary, ERM encompasses a set of processes and methods that give enterprises the ability to manage risks affecting all their functional areas within a holistic and coherent system aimed at ensuring strategic success understood as the ability to continue as a going concern (Kopia et al., 2017).

As the standard approach to risk management became insufficient and inadequate to deal with the increasing volatility in the business world as a result of globalization and other phenomena fostering the emergence of crises (Quon et al., 2012), in contemporary business management, ERM represents a new paradigm for risk management, which should be strategic in nature, undertaken at all hierarchical levels and in all management domains (Beasley et al., 2005). Consequently, the (processual and functional) integration of risk management with other management systems in an enterprise is extremely important when implementing the ERM concept. In view of this, the following ERM functions can be identified in contemporary companies ('O'Donnell, 2005; Frigo & Anderson, 2011):

- it constitutes the basis for achieving competitive advantage,
- it provides an opportunity to prevent risks and, if they materialize, to respond to them more quickly and effectively,
- it focuses on the optimization of risks, allowing an enterprise to take advantage of opportunities related to risks,

- it aligns an enterprise's risk portfolio with its strategic objectives and stakeholder expectations,
- it raises all employees' awareness of possible risks and preventive actions.

In developing a well-functioning ERM system, the main aspects to be taken into account include the rational planning of resources related to undertaking risk optimization activities (enabling the establishment of risk management priorities), the estimation of the ability to respond to the occurrence of crises (defining tolerance levels based on past experience of dealing with unforeseen events) and the integration of strategic risk management activities with those at the operational level, which should allow for more flexible and shorter response times to negative events (Bogodistov & Wohlgemuth, 2017).

As a result, the implementation of a risk management system in a company, in line with the recommendations of the ERM concept, should result in the company's improved resilience to the occurrence of adverse events, reduced exposure to risk, integration of all organizational units in the pursuit of risk-related objectives, strategic support of managers in making decisions on preventive actions, as well as acceptance and compensation for risks (Fraser & Simkins, 2007).

A standardized risk management system is most often designed and implemented under normal and safe operating conditions; however, it also needs to be tested in the event of crises of a different nature, as risk management is intended to be an effective tool to support an enterprise not only under stable conditions but also under critical ones. Thus, despite the fact that risk management is commonly considered a process of a preventive nature aiming to minimize the possibility of negative events occurring (which represents the best way to anticipate and prevent crises), one of its implicit objectives is also to minimize the scale of negative consequences of such events. Thus, risk management processes, and especially the phases of risk identification and analysis, may prove to be effective tools for streamlining management and improving its efficiency once a crisis has actually occurred. In such circumstances, management does not address the risk of a potential crisis, but takes the form of measures targeted at the risk of negative consequences. Risk management during a crisis can also impact the scale of its consequences.

In crisis situations, therefore, it becomes necessary to trigger cooperation between risk management and crisis management processes. Only a skilful combination of the tools of these two management domains can provide a high probability of surviving a crisis and minimizing its undesirable consequences. Indeed, when confronted with a crisis situation, enterprises must often resort to new methods of dealing with risks, which causes standard versions of risk management systems to evolve into non-standard versions, i.e. versions effective in specific crisis situations and adjusted to their characteristic features, as will be discussed in Section 1.2. The relationship between risk management and crisis management is detailed in Figure 1.2.

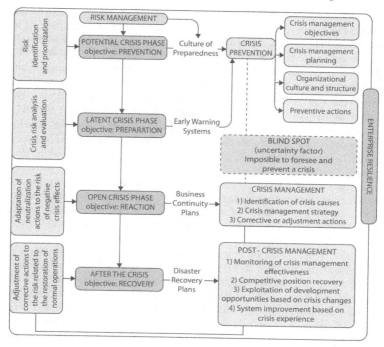

Figure 1.2 Relationship between risk management and crisis management

Source: The authors' own work based on Jedynak and Bąk (2021).

1.2   Non-standard risk management systems

Crises are an inevitable part of the dynamic business world. Unexpected and rapid organizational changes, staffing problems, technological and political changes, as well as changing economic conditions, create instability in the conduct of business. If not identified early and managed properly, a crisis arising in an enterprise as a consequence of such changes can trigger a chain reaction involving the rapid spread of problems throughout the organization and even among its stakeholders (Fener & Cevik, 2015).

It is precisely a crisis situation that generates modifications to standard risk management systems, thus facilitating the development of their non-standard versions. The type, specificity, duration and impact of various crisis situations determine the design, processes and management of non-standard risk management systems.

A crisis in the activities of an enterprise can be defined as an unnatural, complex and unstable situation that poses a threat to its strategic objectives, reputation or survival (PAS 200, 2011). A crisis is a dynamic and progressive process that is never confined to one functional area of an enterprise and its boundaries are blurred. Symptoms of a crisis tend to spread easily throughout an enterprise and beyond (Hart et al., 2001). One current definition of a business crisis indicates that a crisis is an event perceived by managers and stakeholders to be highly significant, unexpected and potentially disruptive, which could prevent an enterprise from achieving its objectives and have serious consequences for its relationships with stakeholders (Bundy et al., 2017). Another definitional approach indicates that a business crisis is a situation that is considered undesirable or harmful and needs to be addressed and overcome. Its severity depends on the intensity of the effects caused and the time required to resolve the problem (Mikušová & Horváthová, 2019). Therefore, irrespective of an enterprise's size or business profile, a crisis constitutes a specific management situation requiring the reorganization of business processes, the implementation of adaptation mechanisms, extensive corrective and remedial actions or actions aimed at limiting the scale of its negative and irreversible consequences.

The situation faced by enterprises during a crisis requires managers to first identify the problem at the occurrence of its very first symptoms or early signs. Once the risks are identified, top management is faced with the challenge of assessing to what extent the possible effects of the crisis will impinge on their company's strategic objectives (whether there will be constraints on its ability to achieve them). Another task is the development of methodologies for dealing with a crisis, to be followed by their phased implementation combined with the ongoing monitoring of their effectiveness (Tutar, 2007). Every crisis disrupts intra-organizational relationships and organizational culture to some extent. The responsibility of leaders and managers is to contain the chaos that is often the first reaction to a crisis, to adapt their enterprise to the changes forced by the crisis, including modifications to the risk management system, and to motivate all employees to make a concerted effort to combat the crisis (Cener, 2007).

A crisis spreading through a company that can be regarded as a problem transforming into a strategic crisis has several characteristic features. These include, for example, the loss of the business management system's ability to self-regulate. Another symptom of the strategic dimension of a crisis is an abrupt slowdown or complete stoppage of an enterprise's further development under crisis circumstances. A third and highly significant manifestation of a crisis reaching its strategic potential is the malfunctioning of basic business mechanisms (Shiller, 2012; Groh, 2014). Crises of a strategic nature require a specific management approach. Such crises, which threaten an enterprise's core functions, require close coordination between the existing strategy, vision and mission and the changes necessitated by the occurrence of a crisis. Such coordination creates opportunities for a transition to a new, post-crisis and sustainable system. The strategic nature of a crisis also requires strategic responses. Such strategic responses include (Wenzel et al., 2020) retrenchment, persevering, innovating and exit.

The experience of past crises should, therefore, be a moment for an enterprise to review its strategy and make necessary changes to it (Bayazit et al., 2003). Furthermore, previously established strategic objectives should influence the shape and scope of measures aimed at preventing potential crises. Therefore, the areas of crisis management, strategic management and risk management should continuously cooperate with each other on a feedback basis.

Every crisis, regardless of the impact it will have on an enterprise, should provide an impulse to learn lessons, draw conclusions and, on the basis of these, improve the enterprise. Such an impulse naturally triggers a series of organizational changes and redefinitions of previously established risk management mechanisms. Their implicit aim is either to return the enterprise to its pre-crisis equilibrium (where the crisis brings only large-scale negative effects) or to strengthen its growth (where the core business is left intact). It is worth remembering, however, that there is no ideal, one-size-fits-all standard for coordinating risk and change management activities during and after a crisis or for adapting an enterprise to resulting changes. The development of a tailor-made system, adapted to the needs of an individual enterprise, is a long-term, methodologically advanced process requiring close integration with strategic management because a crisis itself is regarded as a strategic change.

Looking for post-crisis equilibrium by means of consistently implemented organizational changes requires that the change environment be modelled by the risk management system in order to achieve the highest possible degree of adaptation, which in the long term can also contribute to increased resilience to subsequent crisis events (Rochet et al., 2008). To this end, enterprises in different sectors often use tools originally developed in other management domains, such as change management or lean management (Bąk, 2021; Bąk, 2022).

In the process of adapting the risk management system when confronted with a crisis situation, enterprise managers should take into account the following aspects: (1) modelling the course of a crisis, with a particular focus on post-crisis actions, aiming at not only restoring the normal pre-crisis functioning of an enterprise, but also preventing future crises (Pedersen & Ritter, 2020), thanks to improved risk management systems and resilience mechanisms; (2) exploring relationships among enterprises within business networks, mainly to assess network resilience to crisis (Håkansson & Ford, 2002); (3) increasing employee autonomy, which can translate into faster responses and greater creativity in dealing with dynamic and unexpected changes (Pedersen, 2019); (4) digitizing communication channels used in all business management processes during a crisis, which can result in increased resilience of business models in relation to competitors (Ritter & Pedersen, 2020).

It can therefore be concluded that crisis management is an integral part of a risk management system or a comprehensive approach to risks inherent in the activities of a particular company. Thus, it is important to remember that crisis management cannot be limited to proactive anti-crisis measures. One of its objectives should also be to anticipate the future, with the aim of preventing crises from occurring or preparing an enterprise for their possible occurrence. Moreover, as one of the main management domains, crisis management cannot be limited to episodic activities, either. It should be a continuous process, firmly embedded in an enterprise's management system, compatible with risk management at the prevention stage and with business continuity management at the counteraction stage (e.g. as part of the development of business continuity plans in the event of a crisis).

The sources of threats to enterprises are very diverse. Therefore, crisis prevention and management processes should start with the identification of key risks and their prioritization in view of a particular situation. In a situation where a crisis has already developed, the tailoring of corrective and neutralizing actions must therefore not proceed haphazardly, but in a manner targeted at specific areas of activities where the severity of impact is likely to be greatest. If an enterprise has in place an effective risk management system, which is continuously improved in response to changes in the environment and is oriented towards the areas most susceptible to absorbing the negative effects of crises, the crisis management process becomes optimally effective, rapid and adequate for the character of changes taking place in the enterprise. However, what must be taken into account in each case is the aspect of uncertainty, unavoidable in risk management, i.e. the possibility of extremely unpredictable events of a nature and course that cannot be assessed in advance, such as the COVID-19 pandemic.

In crisis management, it is also extremely important to develop a crisis profile using quantitative and qualitative methods based on the risk profile of a specific enterprise. The construction of a crisis profile aims to identify possible vulnerabilities and identify an enterprise's weaknesses and should consist of the following activities: the identification of sources of potential crises, categorization of crises to which an enterprise may be vulnerable, determination of the probability and time of occurrence, as well as duration of selected types of crises (Mikušová & Horváthová, 2019). Such activities can be important in creating resilience mechanisms for an enterprise.

The COVID-19 pandemic was a source of unique types of crisis experienced with various intensities by enterprises from many different sectors from the beginning of 2020. Consequently, it was not a neutral force for business management systems (Jedynak & Bąk, 2021). During the pandemic, enterprises were forced to adapt their management processes to significantly different conditions for conducting business activities (Li et al., 2021). At the same time, the identification, analysis and assessment of the risks caused by COVID-19 were significantly hampered by the intensity, dynamism and unpredictability of the social and economic changes generated by the pandemic. The characteristic feature of these risks was the difficulty of applying preventive measures and therefore also the inability to implement a preventive strategy (Jedynak & Bąk, 2021) and to exploit the potential of risk management systems that had been developed and proven to work before the pandemic. These systems had to be quickly modified and adapted to the completely new realities of the pandemic.

The COVID-19 pandemic had a not inconsiderable impact on many aspects of the functioning of enterprises in various sectors, including their strategies, organizational cultures, roles and responsibilities, compliance with formal and legal requirements and resilience to threats and crises (Bąk & Jedynak, 2023). The changes that the pandemic induced in enterprises modified their level of exposure to particular risks, as these changes were associated with fundamental uncertainty (Shengelia, 2021) and constituted a consequence of operating in a dynamic risk environment (Li & Ashkanasy, 2019). Therefore, the number of high-risk enterprises increased significantly during the pandemic (Li et al., 2022) and profound transformations in the business ecosystem associated with radical shifts in the boundary conditions between business and society were observed (Anker, 2021). A reconfiguration of the relationship between states and markets was also noted, which directly impacted changes in the area of sectoral risks and risks faced by individual enterprises (Amankwah-Amoah et al., 2021).

The risks that most severely affected companies during the pandemic were mainly financial risks (including liquidity, insurance, pricing, credit risks), organizational risks (including formal and legal risks, personnel risks), strategic risks (including business continuity, reputation, investment risks) and global risks (including global supply chains, technological risks) (Jedynak & Bąk, 2021). It is also important to indicate a notable difference between the impact of pandemic-related changes on the risk structure of small and large enterprises in the same sectors (Cao & Ren, 2022). Small businesses, especially in developing countries, were more severely affected during the pandemic by reduced revenue, lost jobs, life slowing down and weak marketing performance (Engidaw, 2022).

The dominant problem for economies and businesses caused by the COVID-19 pandemic was an economic slowdown of an unprecedented nature. In the SME sector, for example, this slowdown resulted in an intensification of market, economic, financial and operational risks, among which the key risk factors were intense competition and problems with turning a profit (Grondys et al., 2021).

One of the most important areas of risk during the pandemic was technological changes characterized by the dynamic, often forced digitization of operations and the application of artificial intelligence (AI) (Drydakis, 2022).

The pandemic was also a real threat to the financial resilience of businesses, affecting solvency levels, problems with customer acquisition, production and labour costs and deteriorating access to sources of financing (Kaya, 2022). It also contributed to unpredictable changes in employment levels, as well as the values of stock, bonds, commodities and currencies. The consequences of these changes in financial markets caused business models of leading enterprises to collapse (Schoenfeld, 2020).

Another very important, high-risk area of business activity was changes in customer behaviour, preferences and purchasing capabilities. Particularly prominent changes in this area were seen in the sectors of tourism, trade, higher education, etc. (Donthu & Gustafsson, 2020).

In the area of manufacturing, trade and other business operations related to supply and transport, the pandemic multiplied the risks associated with the operation of global supply chains. In this area of business activity, the pandemic is regarded as a black swan phenomenon (Pisz & Kauf, 2022).

In summary, the COVID-19 pandemic had a notable impact on the structure of risks faced by enterprises during the escalation of the crisis situation, but it also significantly affected their future, especially in the areas of the market, financial and personal risks (Dvorský et al., 2021). Indeed, the post-pandemic reality will never be the same as its pre-pandemic counterpart.

All aforementioned modifications in the area of risk exposure in the aftermath of the pandemic can be attributed to the changes it triggered in the global risk landscape, particularly in the area of technological, social, geopolitical, environmental and economic risks (Bąk & Jedynak, 2022).

It is also important to note that not all enterprises experienced a negative increase in risk exposure during the pandemic, thus becoming losers of the pandemic. There were also sectors whose representatives took advantage of growth opportunities during that time by exploiting the potential offered by positive risks, thus becoming winners of the pandemic (Jedynak & Bąk, 2021).

Bibliography

Amankwah-Amoah, J., Khan, Z., Wood, G. (2021). COVID-19 and Business Failures: The Paradoxes of Experience, Scale, and Scope for Theory and Practice. European Management Journal, 39(2), 179–184. DOI: 10.1016/j.emj.2020.09.002

Anker, T.B. (2021). At the Boundary: Post-COVID Agenda for Business and Management Research in Europe and Beyond. European Management Journal, 39(2), 171–178. DOI: 10.1016/j.emj.2021.01.003

Bayazit, Z.D., Cengel, O., Tepe, F.F. (2003). Crisis Management in Organizations and a Case Study. 11th National Management and Organization Congress Leaflet of Notices. Afyon, pp. 366–377.

Bąk, D. (2021). Lean Management w Jednostkach Opieki Zdrowotnej – Cele, Procesy, Efekty Implementacji Lean Management in Health Care Units – Objectives, Processes, Implementation Effects. Medycyna Ogólna i Nauki o Zdrowiu, 27(4), 488–496. DOI: 10.26444/monz/143861

Bąk, D. (2022). Metody i Narzędzia Lean Management w Zarządzaniu Szpitalem – Studia Przypadków. Zdrowie Publiczne i Zarządzanie, 20(2), 34–46. DOI: 10.4467/20842627OZ.22.008.17641

Bąk, S., Jedynak, P. (2022). The Impact of the COVID-19 Pandemic on the Global Risk Landscape in the Era of SMART WORLD. Management Issues, 20(2), 99–120. DOI: 10.7172/1644-9584.96.5

Bąk, S., Jedynak, P. (2023). Risk Management Maturity: A Multidimensional Model. London, New York: Routledge. DOI: 10.4324/9781003330905

Beasley, M.S., Clune, R., Hermanson, D.R. (2005). Enterprise Risk Management: An Empirical Analysis of Factors Associated With the Extent of Implementation. Journal of Accounting and Public Policy, 24(6), 521–531. DOI: 10.1016/j.jaccpubpol.2005.10.001

Bogodistov, Y., Wohlgemuth, V. (2017). Enterprise Risk Management: A Capability-Based Perspective. The Journal of Risk Finance, 18(3), 234–251. DOI: 10.1108/JRF-10-2016-0131

Bromiley, P., McShane, M., Nair, A., Rustambekov, E. (2015). Enterprise Risk Management: Review, Critique and Research Directions. Long Range Planning, 48(4), 265–276. DOI: 10.1016/j.lrp.2014.07.005

Bundy, J., Pfarrer, M.D., Short, C.E., Coombs, W.T. (2017). Crises and Crisis Management: Integration, Interpretation, and Research Development. Journal of Management, 43(6), 1661–1692. DOI: 10.1177/0149206316680030

Cao, L., Ren, J. (2022). Machine Learning Shows That the Covid-19 Pandemic is Impacting U.S. Public Companies Unequally by Changing Risk Structures. PLOS ONE, 17(6), e0269582. DOI: 10.1371/journal.pone.0269582

Cener, P. (2007). Crisis Management. http://www.danismend.com/ (Access: 23.11.2023).

Christopher, M., Mena, C., Khan, O., Yurt, O. (2011). Approaches to Managing Global Sourcing Risk. Supply Chain Management: An International Journal, 16(2), 67–81. DOI: 10.1108/13598541111115338

D'Arcy, S.P., Brogan, J.C. (2001). Enterprise Risk Management. Journal of Risk Management of Korea, 12(1), 1–24.

Dionne, G. (2013). Risk Management: History, Definition and Critique. Risk Management and Insurance Review, 16(2), 147–166. DOI: 10.1111/rmir.12016

Donthu, N., Gustafsson, A. (2020). Effects of COVID-19 on Business and Research. Journal of Business Research, 117, 284–289. DOI: 10.1016/j.jbusres.2020.06.008

Drydakis, N. (2022). Artificial Intelligence and Reduced SMEs' Business Risks. A Dynamic Capabilities Analysis During the COVID-19 Pandemic. Information Systems Frontiers, 24, 1223–1247. DOI: 10.1007/s10796-022-10249-6

Dvorský, J., Čepel, M., Kotásková, M., Bugánová, K. (2021). Differences in Business Risk Effects on the Future of SMEs Due to Covid-19 Pandemic. International Journal of Entrepreneurial Knowledge, 9(2), 14–31. DOI: 10.37335/ijek.v9i2.144

Elahi, E. (2013). Risk Management: The Next Source of Competitive Advantage. Emerald, 15(2), 117–131. DOI: 10.1108/14636681311321121

Engidaw, A.E. (2022). Small Businesses and Their Challenges During COVID-19 Pandemic in Developing Countries: In the Case of Ethiopia. Journal of Innovation and Entrepreneurship, 11(1), 1–14. DOI: 10.1186/s13731-021-00191-3

Fener, T., Cevik, T. (2015). Leadership in Crisis Management: Separation of Leadership and Executive Concepts. Procedia Economics and Finance, 26, 695–701. 10.1016/S2212-5671(15)00817-5

Fischer, K., Leidel, K., Riemann, A., Alfen, H.W. (2010). An Integrated Risk Management System (IRMS) for PPP Projects. Journal of Financial Management of Property and Construction, 15(3), 260–282. DOI: 10.1108/13664381011087515

Fraser, J.R.S., Simkins, B.J. (2007). Ten Common Misconceptions about Enterprise Risk Management. Journal of Applied Corporate Finance, 19(4), 75–81. DOI: 10.1111/j.1745-6622.2007.00161.x

Frigo, M., Anderson, R.J. (2011). Strategic Risk Management: A Foundation for Enterprise Risk Management and Governance. Journal of Corporate Accounting & Finance, 22(3), 81–88. DOI: 10.1002/jcaf.20677

Groh, M. (2014). Strategic Management in Times of Crisis. American Journal of Economics and Business Administration, 6(2), 49–57. DOI: 10.3844/ajebasp.2014.49.57

Grondys, K., Ślusarczyk, O., Hussain, H. I., Androniceanu, A. (2021). Risk Assessment of the SME Sector Operations during the COVID-19 Pandemic. International Journal of Environmental Research and Public Health, 18(8), 4183. DOI: 10.3390/ijerph18084183

Håkansson, H., Ford, D. (2002). How Should Companies Interact in Business Networks? Journal of Business Research, 55(2), 133–139. DOI: 10.1016/S0148-2963(00)00148-X

Hart, P., Heyse, L., Boin, A. (2001). New Trends in Crisis Management Practice and Crisis Management Research: Setting the Agenda. Journal of Contingencies and Crisis Management, 9(4), 181–199. DOI: 10.1111/1468-5973.00168

Jedynak, P., Bąk, S. (2021). Risk Management in Crisis: Winners and Losers During the COVID-19 Pandemic. London, New York: Routledge. DOI: 10.4324/9781003131366

Kaya, O. (2022). Determinants and Consequences of SME Insolvency Risk During the Pandemic. Economic Modelling, 115, 105958. DOI: 10.1016/j.econmod.2022.105958

Kopia, J., Just, V., Geldmacher, W., Bubian, A. (2017). Meaning and Usage of a Conceptual Enterprise Risk Management Framework – A Case Study. EcoForum, 6(2), 1–10.

Li, X., Cheng, B., Li, Y., Duan, J., Tian, Y. (2022). The Relationship between Enterprise Financial Risk and R&D Investment under the Influence of the COVID-19. Frontiers in Public Health, 10, 910758. DOI: 10.3389/fpubh.2022.910758

Li, Y., Ashkanasy, N.M. (2019). Risk Adaptation and Emotion Differentiation: An Experimental Study of Dynamic Decision-Making. Asia Pacific Journal of Management, 36(1), 219–243. DOI: 10.1007/s10490-017-9559-3

Li, J.-Y., Sun, R., Tao, W., Lee, Y. (2021). Employee Coping with Organizational Change in the Face of a Pandemic: The Role of Transparent Internal Communication. Public Relations Review, 47(1), 101984. DOI: 10.1016/j.pubrev.2020.101984

Mikušová, M., Horváthová, P. (2019). Prepared for a Crisis? Basic Elements of Crisis Management in an Organization. Economic Research-Ekonomska Istraživanja, 32(1), 1844–1868. DOI: 10.1080/1331677X.2019.1640625

O'Donnell, E. (2005). Enterprise Risk Management: A System-Thinking Framework for the Event Identification Phase. International Journal of Accounting Information Systems, 6, 177–195. DOI: 10.1016/j.accinf.2005.05.002

PAS 200. (2011). Crisis management – Guidance and good practice. British Standard Institution, London.

Pedersen, C.L. (2019). The 3 Myths of Employee Autonomy. The European Business Review, November/December, pp. 60–63.

Pedersen, C.L., Ritter, T. (2020). Preparing Your Business for a Post-Pandemic World. Harvard Business Review. https://hbr.org/2020/04/preparing-your-business-for-a-post-pandemic-world (Access: 13.04.2020).

Pisz, I., Kauf, S. (2022). Risk and Uncertainty in Supply Chains as a Consequence of COVID-19 Pandemic. Central European Review of Economics & Finance, 38(3), 78–98. DOI: 10.24136/ceref.2022.013

Quon, T.K., Zeghal, D., Maingot, M. (2012). Enterprise Risk Management and Firm Performance. Procedia – Social and Behavioral Sciences, 62, 263–267. DOI: 10.1016/j.sbspro.2012.09.042

Ritter, T., Pedersen, C.L. (2020). Digitization Capability and the Digitalization of Business Models in Business-to-Business Firms: Past, Present, and Future. Industrial Marketing Management, 86(4), 180–190. DOI: 10.1016/j.indmarman.2019.11.019

Rochet, C., Keramidas, O., Bout, L. (2008). Crisis as Change Strategy in Public Organizations. International Review of Administrative Sciences, 74(1), 63–76. DOI: 10.1177/0020852307085734

Schiller, F., Prpich, G. (2012). Learning to Organise Risk Management in Organizations: What Future for Enterprise Risk Management? Journal of Risk Research, 17(8), 999–1017. DOI: 10.1080/13669877.2013.841725

Schoenfeld, J. (2020). The Invisible Business Risk of the COVID-19 Pandemic. https://cepr.org/voxeu/columns/invisible-business-risk-covid-19-pandemic (Access: 16.04.2023).

Shengelia, T. (2021). Perspectives of Small Business Development Under the Conditions of Uncertainty Caused by COVID Pandemics. Globalization and Business, 11, 77–82. DOI: 10.35945/gb.2021.12.010

Shiller, R.J. (2012). The Subprime Solution: How Today's Global Financial Crisis Happened and What to Do About It (1st ed.). Illustrated. Princeton: Princeton University Press.

Sobel, P.J., Reding, K.F. (2004). Aligning Corporate Governance with Enterprise Risk Management. Management Accounting Quarterly, 5(2), 1–9.

Tutar, H. (2007). Management in States of Crisis and Stress (2nd ed.). Istanbul. https://scholar.google.com/scholar?q=Tutar%2C%20H.%2C%20(2007).%20Management%20in%20States%20of%20Crisis%20and%20Stress.%20Second%20Edition.%20Istanbul.p.85.

Wenzel, M., Stanske, S., Lieberman, M.B. (2020). Strategic Responses to Crisis. Strategic Management Journal, 41, 7–18. DOI: 10.1002/smj.3161

2   Risk mitigation

2.1   Types of mitigation actions

Risk mitigation is defined as a purpose action taken by management to counteract in advance the effects of risk materialization and its impact on an enterprise's business operations (Franch et al., 2015). Meanwhile, another definition indicates that risk mitigation is a way of detecting potential problems and responding to them before stakeholders experience their negative consequences (Sebastian-Coleman, 2022).

There is an apparent tendency in business management to decide on the character of risk-mitigating measures based on managers' intuition or external experts' opinions (Hsiao et al., 2013). This approach must be considered valid, but incomplete. Besides managers' and consultants' subjective approach, mitigating actions for individual risks should also be designed on the basis of detailed estimates and simulations resulting from the continuous monitoring of risks carried out within the scope of the risk management system.

The first form of the categorization of risk mitigation actions was the formulation of mitigation strategies. The development of a risk mitigation strategy involves the process of deciding which risks an enterprise should actively counteract and which methods are optimal for this purpose. Inputs necessary for the development of this type of strategy include reports specifying the types of identified risks, the results of analyses and assessments of the individual risks to which an enterprise is exposed, the results of analyses of an enterprise's vulnerability to individual risks, the results of measurements of the probability of individual risks and the results of assessments of the potential impact of individual risks on business operations. The compilation of these inputs enables managers to build risk profiles of individual enterprises and make right decisions on the selection of a risk mitigation strategy appropriate to a given situation (Snedaker & Rima, 2014). Thus, it can be concluded that risk mitigation strategies are methodically conceptualized action plans aimed at reducing the likelihood of the occurrence of risks and neutralizing vulnerabilities that may threaten an enterprise's business performance. Such plans should set out appropriate, well thought out

DOI: 10.4324/9781003514534-2

and tested responses to the occurrence of each risk factor identified by an enterprise. The results of tests and actual applications of such responses should be monitored, recorded and used to improve the risk management system (Ahmed, 2017).

There are different types of business risk mitigation actions, but all can be categorized into the following four strategies (Franch et al., 2015):

- avoid the risk – understood as avoiding actions that may generate risks,
- accept the risk – understood as consciously undertaking risky actions with either complete or incomplete knowledge of the consequences they may entail,
- transfer the risk – understood as taking actions aimed at transferring a risk to other entities such as insurance companies,
- reduce the risk – understood as taking actions to reduce the likelihood of a risk occurring or to reduce the scale of the negative consequences of its materialization.

The strategy for risk mitigation planning is slightly different from the strategies mentioned above. It is extremely important for prioritizing corrective actions within the scope of enterprise-wide risk management functions (Metheny, 2017).

Besides risk mitigation strategies, another form of categorizing risk mitigation actions is their division according to thematic clusters based on individual risk to be mitigated (for example mitigation actions to reduce risks regarding organizational efficiency, mitigation actions to reduce risks regarding requirements, mitigation actions to reduce technological risks, mitigation actions to reduce risks regarding general project management efficiency, etc.) (Shafqat et al., 2022).

Nowadays, managing their risks, enterprises often use the concept of Prioritizing Risk Mitigation, whose main objective is to make every effort to prevent risks from occurring. This prevention should be the leading objective for both an enterprise and its key stakeholders. The application of the Prioritizing Risk Mitigation concept is often accompanied by the use of tools based on innovation and new technologies (D'Addario, 2013).

In order to comprehensively classify mitigation actions introduced in an enterprise in relation to the individual risks to which it is exposed, in our opinion, two classification criteria should be taken into account, namely: (1) an enterprise's approach to individual risks (expressed in the form of its risk mitigation strategy), and (2) risk mitigation management phases. The specific risk mitigation strategy determines which phases of risk mitigation management should be implemented for a given risk factor, while the risk mitigation management process determines which risks should be taken into account at each stage of the process: selected risks, key risks or all risks. Our classification system for risk mitigation actions is presented in Figure 2.1.

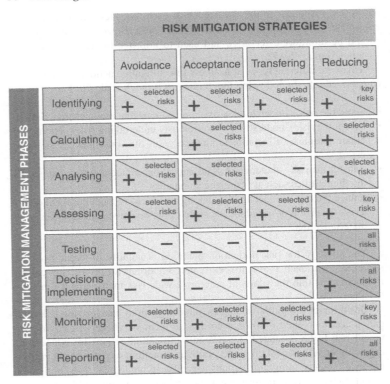

Figure 2.1 A classification system for risk mitigation actions

Source: The authors' own work.

2.2   Risk mitigation actions in crisis situations

Risk mitigation actions implemented in crisis situations often have different characteristics from those implemented in non-crisis conditions. When implementing such measures during a crisis, the timing and dynamics of decision-making properties are often of key importance. Therefore, it is essential that mitigation actions be planned, calculated and tested under an enterprise's normal operating conditions in the event of various hypothetical crisis situations.

Consequently, when planning and developing risk mitigation actions for crisis situations, enterprises should apply the following four cardinal principles (Menoni & Schwarze, 2020):

- adopting an approach taking into account different crisis scenarios,
- precisely estimating the effectiveness and cost-benefit ratio of the adaptation of the planned mitigation actions,

- refining and tailoring mitigation actions to the context and characteristics of a crisis situation,
- strengthening communication processes and treating them as a pillar of the effectiveness of mitigation actions.

In the process of managing a crisis situation, an important aspect is to measure the effectiveness of risk mitigation actions, both those known before the crisis and new ones generated only during the course of the crisis. The key aspect of such measurement is the selection of methods and tools that allow for a reliable assessment of whether the mitigation actions actually implemented are having the desired effect. Well-chosen measurement methods and tools should, firstly, allow for a qualitative assessment of the impact of individual mitigation actions on the core functions of an enterprise during a crisis (de Bruin et al., 2020). Secondly, measurement methods need to be continuously updated in order to ensure their adequacy vis-à-vis dynamic changes that often accompany a crisis. This is because such an update makes it possible to mitigate the effects of a crisis more effectively and to increase the degree of preparedness and sufficiency of an enterprise's response to the occurrence of such effects.

Risk mitigation strategies adopted by enterprises in crisis situations also differ from those developed and applied in stable business conditions. There are a number of key aspects that should be taken into account when risk mitigation actions (used as part of risk management) evolve into actions that mitigate the manifestations of a crisis (used as part of crisis management). These aspects primarily include the following (Vadali, 2023):

- a strong commitment to communication and cooperation with stakeholders,
- strategic decisions on resource allocation,
- mitigation of the financial impact of crisis-related changes,
- synchronization and synergy of the work of risk management teams (focused on risk prevention and mitigation) with crisis management teams (focused on immediate responses and recovery efforts),
- strengthening of an enterprise's resilience through expenditure on anticipating and assessing the impact of risk materialization and the adequacy of implemented mitigation actions.

Risk mitigation processes also play an important role in the Disaster Management Cycle, a concept often used in the management of enterprises during severe and disaster-like crises. The Disaster Management Cycle is designed to support disaster risk management processes and consists of four leading stages: preparedness, response, recovery, and mitigation (Tay, 2022). It is in the last phase of the cycle (mitigation) that efforts generated to prevent disaster risks and impacts play a special role. However, the process of risk mitigation has a slightly different dimension in this concept. It provides for the use of experience gained from a past crisis with the hallmarks of a disaster in order, firstly, to protect an enterprise as much as possible from similar risks in the future and, secondly, to better prepare an enterprise for the consequences of similar threats when their materialization cannot be prevented. In summary, when an enterprise is confronted with a catastrophic crisis, and generally after such a crisis is over, it is advisable to use risk mitigation measures to strengthen an enterprise's culture of preparedness and resilience based on the experience of past crises or disasters.

A specific type of crisis, the COVID-19 pandemic generated specific requirements for mitigation measures implemented by business organizations in the face of emerging new, previously unknown risks. Because businesses and national economies showed great vulnerability to changes in the aftermath of the pandemic and because defence mechanisms developed prior to the pandemic proved ineffective (Eylemer & Kirkpinar Özsoy, 2021), risk management, crisis management and resilience management procedures had to be dynamically redefined during the pandemic.

Consequently, enterprises in various sectors took comprehensive measures to neutralize, minimize or optimize the impact of the pandemic, the main feature of which was the coordination of the management of various risks (Basak & Zhou, 2020). It became a very common activity among companies to look for ways to reduce financial risks (Li et al., 2022), often by implementing financial innovations as a mitigating factor (Kaya, 2022). Another crucial orientation involved selecting and implementing appropriate behavioural models that allow enterprises to make profits despite the pandemic crisis. The implementation of such models was made possible thanks to an appropriate adaptation of corporate culture with the long-term goal of minimizing strategic risks (Engelhardt & White, 2021; Polinkevych et al., 2021).

A very important aspect of risk mitigation efforts during the pandemic was the approach used by many companies, aimed at balancing the needs of an enterprise with its responsibility for ensuring safe working conditions for employees, as demonstrated by the massive shift to remote or hybrid working (Sneddon, 2021).

The implementation of new technological solutions and innovations also became important. During the pandemic, the use of AI-based innovations was becoming increasingly popular, and this trend continues in the post-pandemic period. Most often, such solutions turned out to function well in core services such as marketing and sales, pricing and cash flow, and in facilitating HR activities, which, in addition to bringing obvious benefits, involved changes in business risk (Drydakis, 2022).

Agile responses to changing consumer demand and product supply were also of considerable importance in the protective measures implemented against pandemic-related risks (Zhang, 2023).

As part of the predominant risk mitigation actions during the pandemic, enterprises applied new corporate governance principles (Belas et al., 2021), used protection mechanisms offered by state governments (Engidaw, 2022), increased the resilience of supply chains ('Gatenholm & Halldórsson, 2022; Ma'ady et al., 2022; Modgil et al., 2022), introduced new portfolio of management strategies (Louaas & Picard, 2023), improved workplace safety procedures (Reineholm et al., 2023), pursued digital transformation (Bai et al., 2021; Bettiol et al., 2022), redesigned organizational relationship models (Li et al., 2021) and redefined the leadership role (Thürmer et al., 2020; Koekemoer et al., 2021).

Risk management systems in the post-pandemic reality should therefore be improved and adapted to the new circumstances and the reconstruction of Enterprise Risk Management (ERM), in particular its integrated, strategic and value-enhancing orientation (Pagach & Wieczorek-Kosmala, 2020). They should also enable the identification of strategic assets and be fully integrated into business continuity management (Akmal & Dahlan, 2022), so that the monitoring of risks allows for the implementation of adequate responses (Margherita & Heikkilä, 2021; Lim-u-sanno et al., 2022). Indeed, besides combating the entrenched effects of a pandemic, it is important to build advanced resilience and to ensure business continuity even in crisis conditions, for example by ensuring an agile costbase, optimizing the supply chain to mitigate risk, increasing worker flexibility, as well as enhancing digitization and automation protected by cyber security (Assibi, 2022). These actions should be tailored to both the profile of a given enterprise and the sectoral risk management framework (Grewal et al., 2022).

Considering all the aforementioned areas of risk mitigation measures implemented by companies during the pandemic, it is important to continuously strive to improve the maturity of implemented risk management processes (Bąk & Jedynak, 2023) and to adapt them to the current risk profile of a given enterprise.

Bibliography

Ahmed, R. (2017). Risk Mitigation Strategies in Innovative Projects. In: Key Issues for Management of Innovative Projects. B.L Moya, M.D Storch de Gracia L.F. Mazadiego (eds.), DOI: 10.5772/intechopen.69004

Akmal, M. A., Dahlan, A. R. A. (2022). Integrated Risk Management in the Digital and Pandemic Era. Journal of Information Systems and Digital Technologies, 4(1), 199–208. https://journals.iium.edu.my/kict/index.php/jisdt/article/view/277 (Access: 16.04.2023).

Assibi, A. T. (2022). The Role of Enterprise Risk Management in Business Continuity and Resiliency in the Post-COVID-19 Period. Open Access Library Journal, 9(6), 1–19. DOI: 10.4236/oalib.1108642

Bai, C., Quayson, M., Sarkis, J. (2021). COVID-19 Pandemic Digitization Lessons for Sustainable Development of Micro-and Small- Enterprises. Sustainable Production and Consumption, 27, 1989–2001. DOI: 10.1016/j.spc.2021.04.035

Bąk, S., Jedynak, P. (2023). Risk Management Maturity: A Multidimensional Model. London, New York: Routledge. DOI: 10.4324/9781003330905

Basak, B. D., Zhou, Z. (2020). Diffusing Coordination Risk. American Economic Review, 110(1), 271–297. DOI: 10.1257/aer.20171034

Belas, J., Gavurova, B., Dvorsky, J., Cepel, M., Durana, P. (2021). The Impact of the COVID-19 Pandemic on Selected Areas of a Management System in SMEs. Economic Research-Ekonomska Istraživanja, 35(1), 3757–3777. DOI: 10.1080/1331677X.2021.2004187

Bettiol, M., Capestro, M., Di Maria, E., Micelli, S. (2022). Overcoming Pandemic Challenges Through Product Innovation: The Role of Digital Technologies and Servitization. European Management Journal, 40(5), 707–717. DOI: 10.1016/j.emj.2022.05.003

D'Addario, F. J. (2013). Prioritizing Risk Mitigation. In: Influencing Enterprise Risk Mitigation. 2 ed. Security Executive Council, 47–58. DOI: 10.1016/B978-0-12-417233-3.00004-8

de Bruin, Y. B., Lequarre, A.-S., McCourt, J., Clevestig, P., Pigazzani, F., Jeddi, M. Z., Colosio, C., Goulart, M. (2020). Initial Impacts of Global Risk Mitigation Measures Taken During the Combatting of the COVID-19 Pandemic. Safety Science, 128, 104773. DOI: 10.1016/j.ssci.2020.104773

Drydakis, N. (2022). Artificial Intelligence and Reduced SMEs' Business Risks. A Dynamic Capabilities Analysis During the COVID-19 Pandemic. Information Systems Frontiers, 24, 1223–1247. DOI: 10.1007/s10796-022-10249-6

Engelhardt, L., White, A. (2021). Pandemic Response: Risk Planning in Times of a Crisis United International Business Schools in Amsterdam. American Journal of Management, 21(4), 16–30. https://pesquisa.bvsalud.org/global-literature-on-novel-coronavirus-2019-ncov/resource/pt/covidwho-1414296 (Access: 12.04.2023).

Engidaw, A. E. (2022). Small Businesses and Their Challenges During COVID-19 Pandemic in Developing Countries: in the Case of Ethiopia. Journal of Innovation and Entrepreneurship, 11(1), 1–14. DOI: 10.1186/s13731-021-00191-3

Eylemer, S., Kirkpinar Özsoy, N. (2021). The European Union's Response to COVID-19 as an Existential Threat. International Journal of Contemporary Economics and Administrative Sciences, 11(2), 489–515. DOI: 10.5281/zenodo.5831858

Franch, X., Kenett, R. S., Susi, A., Galanis, N., Glott, R., Mancinelli, F. (2015). Community Data for OSS Adoption Risk Management. The Art and Science of Analyzing Software Data, 377–409. DOI: 10.1016/B978-0-12-411519-4.00014-8

Gatenholm, G., Halldórsson, A. (2022). Responding to Discontinuities in Product-Based Service Supply Chains in the COVID-19 Pandemic: Towards Transilience. European Management Journal, 41(3), 425–436. DOI: 10.1016/j.emj.2022.02.007

Grewal, J., Habahbeh, L., Acharyya, M., Aravind, R., Bhagaloo, S., Carey, M., Er, C., Farrugia, K., Leung, K. (2022). COVID-19 and the Effectiveness of ERM Frameworks. British Actuarial Journal, 27, e23. DOI: 10.1017/S1357321722000174

Hsiao, C., Malak, R., Tumer, I. Y., Doolen, T. (2013). Empirical Findings about Risk and Risk Mitigating Actions from a Legacy Archive of a Large Design Organization. Procedia Computer Science, 16, 844–852. DOI: 10.1016/j.procs.2013.01.088

Kaya, O. (2022). Determinants and Consequences of SME Insolvency Risk During the Pandemic. Economic Modelling, 115, 105958. DOI: 10.1016/j.econmod.2022.105958

Koekemoer, L., Beer, L. T., De, Govender, K., Brouwers, M. (2021). Leadership Behaviour, Team Effectiveness, Technological Flexibility, Work Engagement and Performance During COVID- 19 Lockdown: An Exploratory Study. SA Journal of Industrial Psychology, 47, 1–9. DOI: 10.4102/sajip.v47i0.1829

Li, J.-Y., Sun, R., Tao, W., Lee, Y. (2021). Employee Coping With Organizational Change in the Face of a Pandemic: The Role of Transparent Internal Communication. Public Relations Review, 47(1), 101984. DOI: 10.1016/j.pubrev.2020.101984

Li, X., Cheng, B., Li, Y., Duan, J., Tian, Y. (2022). The Relationship Between Enterprise Financial Risk and R&D Investment Under the Influence of the COVID-19. Frontiers in Public Health, 10, 910758. DOI: 10.3389/fpubh.2022.910758

Lim-u-sanno, K., Wiroonratch, B., Boonsong, M. (2022). Influence of Effective Enterprise Risk Management on Performance of Hotels in the COVID-19 Pandemic. Social Space, 22(1), 1–19. https://socialspacejournal.eu/menu-script/index.php/ssj/article/view/14/14 (Access: 16.04.2023).

Louaas, A., Picard, P. (2023). A Pandemic Business Interruption Insurance. The Geneva Risk and Insurance Review, 48, 1–30. DOI: 10.1057/s10713-023-00080-7

Ma'ady, M. N. P., Vanany, I., Mardhiana, H., Albana, A. S. (2022). The Important of Supply Chain Resilience During Covid-19 Pandemic For Enterprise Risk Management: A Systematic Literature Review. Proceedings of the 1st International Conference on Contemporary Risk Studies, ICONIC-RS 2022, 31 March-1 April 2022, South Jakarta, DKI Jakarta, Indonesia. https://eudl.eu/doi/10.4108/eai.31-3-2022.2320664 (Access: 13.04.2023).

Margherita, A., Heikkilä, M. (2021). Business Continuity in the COVID-19 Emergency: A Framework of Actions Undertaken by World-Leading Companies. Business Horizons, 64(5), 683–695. DOI: 10.1016/j.bushor.2021.02.020

Menoni, S., Schwarze, R. (2020). Recovery During a Crisis: Facing the Challenges of Risk Assessment and Resilience Management of COVID-19. Environment Systems and Decisions, 40(2), 189–198. DOI: 10.1007/s10669-020-09775-y

Metheny, M. (2017). Applying the NIST risk management framework. Federal Cloud Computing, 2 edition. The Definitive Guide for Cloud Service Providers, 117–183. DOI: 10.1016/B978-0-12-809710-6.00005-6

Modgil, S., Gupta, S., Stekelorum, R., Laguir, I. (2022). AI Technologies and Their Impact on Supply Chain Resilience During COVID-19. International Journal of Physical Distribution & Logistics Management, 52(2), 130–149. DOI: 10.1108/IJPDLM-12-2020-0434

Pagach, D., Wieczorek-Kosmala, M. (2020). The Challenges and Opportunities for ERM Post-COVID-19: Agendas for Future Research. Journal of Risk and Financial Management, 13(12), 323. DOI: 10.3390/jrfm13120323

Polinkevych, O., Khovrak, I., Trynchuk, V., Klapkiv, Y., Volynets, I. (2021). Business Risk Management in Times of Crises and Pandemics. Montenegrin Journal of Economics, 17(3), 99–110. DOI: 10.14254/1800-5845/2021.17-3.8

Reineholm, C., Ståhl, C., Lundqvist, D. (2023). Bringing Risk Back in: managers' Prioritization of the Work Environment during the Pandemic. International Journal of Workplace Health Management, 16(1), 4–19. DOI: 10.1108/IJWHM-03-2022-0041

Sebastian-Coleman, L. (2022). Core Data Quality Management Capabilities. In: Meeting the Challenges of Data Quality Management, 187–228. DOI: 10.1016/B978-0-12-821737-5.00009-2

Shafqat, A., Oehmen, J., Welo, T., Ringen, G. (2022). The Role of Risk Mitigation Actions in Engineering Projects: An Empirical Investigation. Systems Engineering, 25(6), 584–608. DOI: 10.1002/sys.21639

Snedaker, S., Rima, C. (2014). Risk Assessment. In: Business Continuity and Disaster Recovery Planning for IT Professionals, 2 ed., 151–224. DOI: 10.1016/B978-0-12-410526-3.00004-0

Sneddon, J. (2021). Pandemic risk management; protecting people while ensuring business continuity. American Institute of Chemical Engineers 2021 Spring Meeting and 17th Global Congress on Process Safety, Virtual, April 18-22, 2021. https://aiche.onlinelibrary.wiley.com/doi/full/10.1002/prs.12302 (Access: 13.04.2023).

Tay, H. L. (2022). Mitigating Risks in the Disaster Management Cycle. Advances in Civil Engineering. Special Issue: Frontiers in Disaster Risk Reduction for Sustainable Development, 7454760, DOI: 10.1155/2022/7454760

Thürmer, J. L., Wieber, F., Gollwitzer, P. M. (2020). Management in Times of Crisis: Can Collective Plans Prepare Teams to Make and Implement Good Decisions? Management Decision, 58(10), 2155–2176. DOI: 10.1108/MD-08-2020-1088

Vadali, R. (2023). Risk vs Crisis Management. https://www.linkedin.com/pulse/risk-vs-crisis-management-ramesh-chandran-vadali-udb7f (Access: 15.02.2024).

Zhang, D. (2023). Understanding Enterprise Risk Management of the Retail Industry During the Pandemic-Case Study of Walmart. SHS Web of Conferences, 154, 01018. DOI: 10.1051/shsconf/202315401018

3   Risk profiling

3.1   The essence of a risk profile

So far the literature on the subject has failed to present a coherent and uniform definition of a risk profile. The term is used in various contexts, which will be outlined below. Furthermore, the academic literature does not explain how a risk profiling process should be developed and performed, nor how enterprises could benefit from an ongoing and continuously updated process of profiling the risks they are exposed to.

Some sources define a risk profile as an evaluation of an individual's willingness and ability to take risks (Barone, 2020), i.e. they present a qualitative way of understanding this term. In this sense, a risk profile is regarded as an indicator of an enterprise's ability to cope with different types of threats to which it is exposed. Such an understanding of a risk profile can be important with regard to managing financial risks, for example in determining the appropriate allocation of assets in an investment portfolio. In this case, a risk profile can be used as a tool to help identify ways to mitigate potential risks and threats.

There are also other approaches which present a quantitative way of understanding and using risk profiles in business management. One of them has been proposed by Pratt (2023). In such approaches, a risk profile constitutes a quantitative analysis of the types of threats an organization, asset, project or individual faces. In this sense, the purpose of a risk profile is to provide an objective understanding of risks to which an enterprise is exposed by assigning numerical values to variables representing various risks and dangers posed by them. This allows enterprises to use risk profiles to adapt their strategies to the current level of risk appetite, i.e. the level they are able to accept with the simultaneous application of appropriate control mechanisms.

At this point it is worth emphasizing uniqueness as one of the characteristic features of a risk profile, which means that each business entity has its own individual risk profile depending on its business activities, competitive position, resources, relations with the environment, strategic objectives and ability to counter risks. Moreover, another quality of a risk profile is its

DOI: 10.4324/9781003514534-3

volatility, which means that once developed, a risk profile is impermanent and will fluctuate with changes taking place both within an enterprise and in its environment. This quality can result in a sceptical attitude towards planning and building risk profiles. This is because the process requires adequate, often expert, knowledge, commitment of resources and a great deal of time and expense, and can result in a risk profile that becomes obsolete very quickly even as a result of minor organizational changes, not to mention global crisis situations where enterprises' risk profiles can change dramatically from one day to the next. Nevertheless, the volatility of risk profiles should not discourage managers from building and using them, provided they are updating on an ongoing basis. Only this approach to risk management allows for a high probability of success for previously planned and implemented actions aimed at mitigating risks included in a profile. In our opinion, the mandatory and ongoing updating of a risk profile implies another characteristic, namely flexibility. Enterprises planning to improve their risk management based on the construction of a risk profile should be aware that the key inputs to this process are those resulting from the continuous monitoring of their internal and external environments. Only risk profiles that are flexibly modified in parallel with changes in the environment can constitute a reliable source for planning effective preventive, neutralizing and corrective actions for individual risks.

Any enterprise can be viewed through the prism of its risk profile by a wide range of its internal and external stakeholders. Essentially, each business entity constitutes a bundle of risks, i.e. it can be said that a risk profile is an enterprise's unique "business card". It should therefore present such information as to describe an enterprise in terms of its own individual risk profile. A risk profile should take into account both potentialities of bad (downside) and good (upside) risks. It should also highlight the key risks (sorted on the basis of the probability of their occurrence and/or expected impact on an enterprise (Banasiewicz, 2014). With this approach to building a risk profile, it is possible to compare enterprises (e.g. ones belonging to the same sector) in terms of, for example, investment security, stability of market position, vulnerability to crisis, etc.

Also, a risk profile is not a static concept. On the contrary, it is a dynamic process, or even a set of processes. The risk profiling process is discussed in detail in Section 3.2.

Based on the above considerations, we have developed a catalogue of the main characteristic features of an enterprise risk profile. It is shown in Figure 3.1.

To bridge the gap regarding the lack of a uniform definition of a risk profile, we propose that the concept of a risk profile should be understood as the identification of an enterprise's exposure to specific risk factors, the categorization of these factors, as well as the planning and implementation of actions aimed at mitigating all identified risk factors. Furthermore, a risk profile should include a prioritization of the identified risks made on the basis of two criteria: the likelihood of their occurrence and their expected impact on the enterprise.

Figure 3.1 Characteristics of a risk profile

Source: The authors' own work.

On the basis of this prioritization, it should be possible to select the key risks that require the greatest degree of commitment in terms of their management. An important aspect of a risk profile is also the necessity to update it on an ongoing basis in line with changes taking place in the environment, which we see as particularly relevant during and after crisis situations. The last key aspect of a risk profile is the monitoring of the effectiveness of mitigation actions implemented in response to the risk factors included in the profile.

3.2 The structure of a risk profile

The process of designing, building and using a risk profile in an enterprise's operations (i.e. risk profiling) should be carried out in a methodical, structured manner and based on reliable sources of information.

In our view, a risk profile should emerge as a result of a management process consisting of the following phases:

- planning a risk profile,
- designing the structure of a risk profile,
- preparing to build a risk profile,
- building a risk profile,
- measuring the risk profile,
- assessing the adequacy of the risk profile,
- designing actions to mitigate the risks included in the profile,
- using the risk profile in risk and crisis management,
- implementing the mitigation actions,

- assessing the effectiveness of management decisions based on the risk profile,
- assessing the effectiveness of the mitigation actions,
- continuous monitoring of the environment,
- continuous updating of the risk profile.

A graphical representation of the risk profiling process is shown in Figure 3.2.

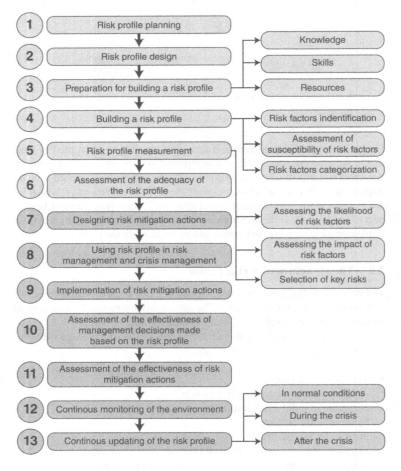

Figure 3.2 Risk profiling
Source: The authors' own work.

The risk profiling process should start with a detailed planning of the structure of a profile. Planning should take into account an enterprise's individual risk management needs, i.e. its business profile, individual situation and competitive position, as well as the sector in which it operates and the current environment.

Taking into consideration the conditions indicated above, an enterprise should carefully design its risk profile, i.e. its scope, shape, tools and metrics to be used in its construction and performance measurement. Furthermore, already at the design phase, enterprise managers should decide to what extent and for what purposes they will use a risk profile in their management processes.

The next step is to prepare for the construction of a risk profile. This preparation should take place with respect to the three dimensions of knowledge, skills and resources. The knowledge needed to build a risk profile is of primary importance. If there is a dedicated risk management unit or function (e.g. risk manager) within an enterprise's organizational structure, it is likely that it will be able to comprehensively build and manage a risk profile on its own. However, if no one in an enterprise is formally responsible for risk management, then external expertise may be necessary. Another issue that has to be taken into consideration in preparations for the construction of a risk profile is the skills of all staff who will be involved in the process and subsequent work related to the functioning of a risk profile. It is possible that individual teams will need specialized training before being allowed to carry out this work. The third issue is related to the availability of resources. This concerns financial, informational and technological resources that, firstly, will make it possible to build a profile and, secondly, can assist in its management, e.g. through the use of technological tools that automate certain processes, facilitate measurement, etc.

The next step is the construction of a risk profile. It requires first of all the identification of all the risks to which an enterprise is and may be exposed at a given moment. This step is followed by an assessment of an enterprise's vulnerability to all identified risk factors. This is often one of the more difficult tasks in the whole process, as vulnerability to risks can be highly variable. Therefore, vulnerability assessments should be carried out regularly. The last task at this stage is to categorize the identified risk factors. The factors should be divided on the basis of a relevant criterion, for example into the factors of operational, strategic, regulatory, technological, business, personnel, etc. risks. Such categorization facilitates the subsequent matching of mitigation actions to the appropriate groups of risk factors.

Once a risk profile is already developed, it should be measured systematically. Firstly, the probability of the occurrence of all risk factors present in a profile and their expected impact on an enterprise should be measured. Based on the results of these measurements, it should be possible to identify the key risks, i.e. those that are most likely to occur and whose impact on an enterprise is likely to be the most severe. The key risks should be managed with the utmost care and commitment, as their actual materialization could cause serious problems, even threatening business continuity.

The next step in the risk profile management process is the measurement of its adequacy. Specifically, it is a matter of adapting the profile adequately to the situation in which the enterprise finds itself at a given time and to the current macroeconomic situation in the sector in which it operates and beyond it. The result of the adequacy measurement should be the starting point for designing risk mitigation actions.

Mitigation actions should be designed for each risk factor identified in a profile, not just the key risks. Enterprises often assume that it is not worth spending resources on measures to mitigate risks that are unlikely to occur. However, such an assumption is incorrect. Mitigation actions should be designed for all risks, without exception. What is more, they should be verified under simulated conditions so that, when an enterprise faces the actual materialization of risks, they have been duly tested and prepared for fully effective implementation.

Built according to the above procedures, a risk profile is at this stage ready for managers to use in functioning risk management and crisis management systems. Previously designed and tested risk mitigation actions are also ready for implementation.

The next step in the risk profiling process comprises verification and control activities. Firstly, the effectiveness of management decisions taken on the basis of the developed risk profile should be assessed. Secondly, the effectiveness of the implemented mitigation measures should also be verified. Thus, it is necessary to check whether the implemented mitigation actions have helped prevent the occurrence of the risks and, if prevention has not been effective, it is necessary to check whether the mitigation actions have reduced the scale and severity of the negative consequences of risk materialization.

The last step in the risk profiling process is the continuous and very detailed monitoring of the environment, changes in the risks to which an enterprise is exposed and its degree of vulnerability to these risks. By doing so, enterprises can maintain their risk profiles up to date and are prepared in advance to deal with problems or crises. Risk profiles should be updated regularly under all conditions: in normal non-crisis conditions, during or after a crisis.

3.3 The roles and functions of risk profiling in business operations

Risk profiling is a process that can bring tangible benefits to enterprises. At the most general level, a risk profile can be considered as a tool that helps enterprises to understand their level of exposure to particular types of risks, to adequately identify the owners of individual risks, to verify what risk management resources are actually being spent on and to estimate their own risk absorption capacity (Jordan, 2013).

The other specific functions fulfilled by the risk profiling process include (Chivers et al., 2009; Hughes, 2015; Ibitola, 2023; Ndeto, 2023):

- proactive risk management (profiling enables managers' active approach to identifying and addressing threats before they become major problems),
- support for decision-making processes (profiling facilitates an understanding of specific risks faced by an enterprise; consequently, managers can make informed decisions, for example, on resource allocation),
- facilitation of communication processes (profiling promotes more effective communication within task teams and between enterprises and their stakeholders),
- opportunities for the development of adequate contingency plans (profiling makes both what is expected of an enterprise and what it itself plans realistic and precise, thus helping an enterprise to accurately design contingency measures),
- accurate allocation of resources (profiling helps to allocate resources efficiently; focusing on the most critical risks, managers are able to reduce losses),
- increased operational efficiency (profiling increases the chances of an enterprise's success due to the elimination of key risks in advance, the planning of highly predictable paths for an enterprise's development, and the raising of both internal and external stakeholders' awareness and satisfaction levels,
- updating of the knowledge of the environment in which an enterprise operates (profiling makes it possible to take adequate decisions in risk management, always adapted to the current internal and external conditions),
- complementation and expansion of opportunities provided by other risk management methods and tools (compared to other methods, profiling significantly expands an enterprise's preventive, corrective and risk neutralizing capabilities),
- exercise of risk management even in volatile and dispersed conditions (profiling enables an assessment of risks to be synchronized with environmental conditions, making the resulting risk management strategies more realistic and always up to date),
- increase of credibility in determining stakeholders' attitudes towards risks (profiling helps to reflect stakeholders' attitudes, preferences and intentions),
- support for risk-related compliance procedures (profiling is a transparent and continuously documented process and therefore reduces the risk of fraudulent decision-making based on data that differ from those included in the profile),
- systematization and analysis of vast amounts of data on risks and threats (thanks to its structured and transparent form, profiling facilitates the processing of all data used to assess an enterprise's exposure to risks and the feasibility of designing mitigation actions),

- enhanced security of an enterprise's operations, transactions and interactions with customers (profiling makes it easier for businesses to navigate the increasingly complex world of digital interactions and transactions, thus increasing the security and integrity of operations).

Besides being useful to enterprises in their general management systems, risk profiling can also be a helpful tool for specific functions, such as project management. In this area, risk profiling is considered a key tool needed to navigate a complex and uncertain environment. This is because systematic identification, assessment, prioritization and development of methods aimed at mitigating risks increase the likelihood of successful project completion. Risk profiling in project management is therefore considered to be a key aspect of strategic planning for project implementation (Ndeto, 2023).

Risk profiling can also be an effective tool for corporate investment management, supporting the achievement of a consistent investment process for all clients (Hughes, 2015) due to the transparency of information on risks and methods implemented to prevent them. Due to the development of risks and threats in the financial sphere, including cyber threats, risk profiling has become an indispensable part of the activities of actors in the financial sector. Through profiling, it is possible to provide a primary line of defence against fraud and other forms of financial crime, thus helping to protect both financial institutions and their customers (Ibitola, 2023).

Bibliography

Banasiewicz, A. (2014). Organizational Risk Profile Measurement and Management. Davos, Switzerland: Global Risk Forum.

Barone, A. (2020). Risk Profile: Definition, Importance for Individuals & Companies. https://www.investopedia.com/terms/r/risk-profile.asp (Access: 17–02.2024).

Chivers, H., Clark, J. A., Cheng, P.-C. (2009). Risk Profiles and Distributed Risk Assessment. Computers & Security, 28(7), 521–535. DOI: 10.1016/j.cose.2009.04.005

Hughes, E. A. (2015). Pros and Cons of Risk Profiling Tools. https://www.ftadviser.com/2015/06/18/ifa-industry/companies-and-people/pros-and-cons-of-risk-profiling-tools-QmBftVvrrc18tmDtEqnmiL/article.html (Access: 18.02–2024).

Ibitola, J. (2023). Risk Profiling Amidst Deceptive Identities. https://www.flagright.com/post/risk-profiling-amidst-deceptive-identities (Access: 18.02.2024).

Jordan, A. (2013). What's Your Risk Profile? https://www.projectmanagement.com/articles/281719/what-s-your-risk-profile-#_=_ (Access: 17.02.2024).

Ndeto, R. (2023). Project Management and Risk Profiling: A Winning Combination. https://www.linkedin.com/pulse/project-management-risk-profiling-winning-combination-ndeto-robert-lec9c (Access: 18.02.2024).

Pratt, M. K. (2023). Risk Profile. https://www.techtarget.com/searchsecurity/definition/risk-profile (Access: 17.02.2024).

4 Research methodology

4.1 Research objectives and questions

We divided the planned research process into the following stages:

1 identification of the research gap,
2 formulation of the objectives and research questions,
3 development of the research methodology,
4 selection of enterprises for the research,
5 selection of empirical data sources,
6 performance of the research,
7 analysis of research results,
8 identification of implications of the obtained research results for theory and practice.

In view of the research gap identified in the literature regarding the deficit of studies on changes in the risk profiles of enterprises as a result of the COVID-19 pandemic, the main objective of our research was to identify the risk profiles of selected enterprises representing the financial, construction and IT sectors before and during the COVID-19 pandemic.

Our specific research objectives included the following:

* to identify changes that took place during the pandemic in terms of exposure to risks identified by the enterprises before the pandemic,
* to identify new risks that emerged in the enterprises' risk profiles as a result of changes resulting from the pandemic,
* to highlight differences and similarities in the enterprises' risk profiles occurring over time (to compare the period before the pandemic with the period during the pandemic), as well as within individual sectors and between them,
* to explore risk mitigation actions put in place by enterprises during the pandemic,
* to identify the practical implications of research aimed at establishing the interdependencies between risk profiling and business resilience.

DOI: 10.4324/9781003514534-4

With respect to the research objectives formulated above, we posed two main research questions (RQs):

RQ1: How did the COVID-19 pandemic affect the risk profiles of the selected enterprises representing the financial, construction and IT sectors?

RQ2: What risk mitigation actions did the enterprises representing the financial, construction and IT sectors implement as a result of the COVID-19 pandemic?

4.2 Data sources

For the research, we qualified 107 companies from the financial, construction and IT sectors, listed on the Warsaw Stock Exchange as at 25 June 2019 (before the pandemic) and also as at 10 September 2021 (during the course of the pandemic). The selection of this particular group was motivated by their listing on the Warsaw Stock Exchange, which makes them formally obliged to identify, monitor and report risks. This formal obligation, in turn, allows for free access to such information included in the companies' publicly available internal documents. The characteristics of the selected enterprises are presented in Table 4.1.

Table 4.1 The enterprises selected for the research

Sector	Sub-sector	Designations of enterprises	Number of enterprises in the sub-sector	Number of enterprises in the sector
Construction (CON)	Construction	CON 1-CON 38	38	38
Financial Services (FS)	Banks	FS 1-FS 12	12	28
	Leasing and factoring	FS 13	1	
	Financial intermediation	FS 14-FS 15	2	
	Capital market	FS 16-FS 21	6	
	Insurance	FS 22-FS 24	3	
	Debt collection	FS 25-FS 28	4	
IT (IT)	Information technology	IT 1-IT 24	24	41
	Media	IT 25-IT 38	14	
	Telecommunication	IT 39-IT 41	3	
Total	-		**107**	**107**

Source: The authors' own work.

The main sources of data were internal documents of the examined enterprises, which included:

- annual reports (financial statements and management reports),
- reports on capital adequacy as well as other information and disclosures subject to obligatory publication by entities listed on the WSE,
- non-financial information statements,
- corporate governance statements,
- integrated reports or sustainability reports.

4.3 Research methods

In the research process, we used a mix-method approach (Bazeley, 2008). Qualitative research methods with the support of selected quantitative tools played a dominant role. The applied research approach was based on a multiple case study in a variant combining both descriptive and exploratory elements (Yin, 2003). In order to identify the risk factors of the examined enterprises, we used the method consisting in analysing the content of their source documentation (Bowen, 2009). Risk factors were identified based on the data of the examined enterprises contained in their internal documents. In order to categorize the identified risk factors, we used a one-dimensional logical classification method, based on a two-level division (risk categories and risk factors included in a category), meeting the required criteria of exhaustiveness and separability (Bailey, 1994; Saran, 2014) – exhaustiveness (all risk factors were included in a substantively adequate category), separability (each risk factor is allocated to only one category). In the next step, we used a quantitative tool in the form of a numerical data analysis (Babbie, 2010; Muijs, 2010) with respect to the frequency of the occurrence of the identified risk factors among the enterprises representing the three sectors, in order to finally build sectoral risk profiles.

We applied the research procedures outlined above to the examined companies in two periods – in the year 2019 on the basis of data for the year 2018 (before the COVID-19 pandemic) and in the year 2022 on the basis of data for the year 2021 (during the course of the COVID-19 pandemic) – to identify changes in the risk profiles caused by the pandemic. For this purpose, we used a comparative approach for comparisons over time (Pennings et al., 2006; Esser & Vliegenthart, 2017).

In order to identify risk mitigation actions implemented in the selected enterprises, we analysed available qualitative data (Gibbs, 2021), including relevant excerpts from the enterprises' documents. For this purpose, we coded the data, using the MAXQDA Analytics Pro 2022 software. We used grounded coding, based on observations made during the course of the research and the obtained research material. It took the form of hierarchical coding, i.e. multilevel coding based on the extraction of the main categories of codes together with the sub-categories assigned to them. The coding approach adopted by us was data driven coding, that is coding based on a close relationship with data and providing for the incremental generation of analytical conclusions (Gibbs, 2007; Gibbs, 2021).

According to methodological rigour, we divided the coding process into the following stages:

- we prepared data for coding (selecting citations from the source documents of the examined enterprises and assigning them to the enterprises based on the adopted numbering within the sectors under examination),
- we performed the first coding cycle (in this cycle, either coder independently conducted the process of coding the citations selected from the enterprises' documentation),
- we prepared the codebook,
- we performed the second coding cycle (on the basis of the codes selected by the coders independently, we identified common codes, relying on the substantive relationships between the codes; we qualified 233 common codes for further analysis; after the final filtering and elimination of synonymous codes, we approved 159 codes for the final analysis),
- the codes were prioritized and categorized, creating a code tree (whereby we organized the codes, created code bundles and hierarchical categories):

  - we created seven main categories of codes,
  - within each of the seven main categories of codes, we established three subcategories, following the principle of separability and exhaustiveness of the created subcategories,
  - to each of the established subcategories, we assigned specific codes based on their relevance,

- we analysed the relationships between the codes and their categories to interpret the results of the research.

Bibliography

Babbie, E. (2010). The Practice of Social Research. 12th edition. Belmont, CA: Wadsworth Cengage.

Bailey, K. D. (1994). Typologies and Taxonomies – An Introduction to Classification Techniques. Thousand Oaks, CA: Sage Publications.

Bazeley, P. (2008). Mixed Methods in Management Research. R. Thorpe & R. Holt (Eds), The SAGE Dictionary of Qualitative Management Research. London: Sage, 133–136.

Bowen, G. A. (2009). Document Analysis as a Qualitative Research Method. Qualitative Research Journal, 9(2), 27–40. DOI: 10.3316/QRJ0902027

Esser, F., Vliegenthart, R. (2017). Comparative Research Methods. J. Matthe (ed.), The International Encyclopedia of Communication Research Methods, London: John Wiley & Sons, 1–22. DOI: 10.1002/9781118901731.iecrm0035

Gibbs, G. (2007). Analyzing Qualitative Data. New York, NY: Sage.

Gibbs, G. (2021). Analizowanie danych jakościowych. Warszawa: PWN.

Muijs, D. (2010). Doing Quantitative Research in Education with SPSS. 2nd edition. London: SAGE Publications. doi: 10.4135/9781446287989

Pennings, P., Keman, H., Kleinnijenhuis, J. (2006). The Comparative Approach: Theory and Method. In: Doing Research in Political Science. Sage. DOI: 10.4135/9781849209038

Saran, J. (2014). Classification and Typologies as Tools for Pedagogical Empirical Research Improvement. Studia i Prace Pedagogiczne, 1, 13–30. Retrieved from https://wydawnictwo.wsei.eu/wp-content/uploads/2020/09/SIPP_1_214.pdf (12.04.2023).

Yin, R. K. (2003). Case Study Research: Design and Methods (3rd ed.). Thousand Oaks, CA: Sage.

5 Impact of the COVID-19 pandemic on the risk profiles of the selected enterprises representing the financial, construction and IT sectors

5.1 Impact of the pandemic on the modification of the risk profiles of the analysed enterprises – A sectoral approach

5.1.1 Financial sector

A comparison of the risk profiles of the examined financial sector companies before and during the COVID-19 pandemic is presented graphically in Figure 5.1.

Compared to before the pandemic, the first change observed during its course concerned the exposure of the examined financial sector companies to individual risk factors. Analysing these changes with respect to the arrangement of risk categories, we observed significant differences in the frequency of their identification. Before the pandemic, all of the examined enterprises (28) had identified financial risks, which had been quite obvious given the nature of the sector, whereas during the pandemic, the most frequently identified risks were not those belonging to the financial categories, but those of a strategic character, as they were identified by 27 of the 28 examined companies. This is a noticeable change in view of the fact that prior to the pandemic, strategic risks had appeared in the risk catalogues of only 19 of the 28 examined enterprises. Also noteworthy is the increase in importance of personal and technological risks in the sector during the pandemic.

Conducting a more detailed analysis of the changes in risk exposure, i.e. with regard to specific risk factors from the respective categories, we also noted significant changes brought about by the pandemic. The most significant of those included a marked increase in exposure to the financial result risk (B2), the legal risk (REG2), the risk of radical changes in the business environment (S1), the risk of changes in macroeconomic conditions (S2) and the cyber security risk (T1). The examined companies pointed out that the pandemic had a significant impact on the above aspects of their business activities. For example, the company FS24 indicated that: "Service provision is based on the conduct of pre-judicial and judicial proceedings, which may be significantly prolonged as a result of external circumstances such as the COVID-19 pandemic". Company

DOI: 10.4324/9781003514534-5

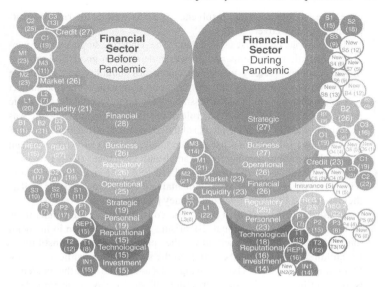

Figure 5.1 The risk profiles of the examined financial sector companies before and during the pandemic

Note: The results of the research on which the figure is based can be found in Appendix 5.1 at the end of this chapter.

Source: The authors' own work.

FS20 assessed that "macroeconomic problems caused a change in our business model due to the continuation of the COVID-19 pandemic".

Our most important research achievement, however, is the identification of new risks that emerged during the COVID-19 pandemic and had not been earlier taken into account by the examined enterprises. Completely new elements emerged in the categories of financial (4), strategic (5), business (1), operational (3), personnel (3), technological (1) and investment (1) risks. In total, we identified 18 new risks that occurred in the sector during the pandemic and were its direct or indirect consequences. Interestingly, during the pandemic some of the companies (13 out of 28) started to recognize a new risk (S8), and categorized it as strategic. In their own words: "The main risk we face, similarly to the global economy, is the SARS-CoV-2 pandemic" (FS7) or "The most important of the risks remains the COVID-19 pandemic and its subsequent waves" (FS20, FS23, FS24). Other new risks that showed direct links to the impact of the pandemic were the following:

- among financial risks: the risk of deterioration in borrowers' creditworthiness (C4), the risk related to forbearance practices (C5), the risk of excessive indebtedness and insolvency (L3), as well as the risk of insufficient insurance coverage (I1).

For example, enterprises stated that: "The pandemic surge and new pandemic restrictions are hampering growth in demand for goods and services in the economy, thereby worsening companies' liquidity and increasing their credit risk" (FS3), so "the customer and transactions must be subject to a comprehensive credit risk assessment taking into account the economic impact of COVID-19" (FS4). The role of insurance during a pandemic was also highlighted: "One of the effects of the pandemic is also a higher level of customer awareness and a sense of uncertainty, which is associated with an expected increase in demand for life and health insurance" (FS23).

- among strategic risks: the institutional risk (S4), the risk of cooperation with stakeholders (S5), the environmental and climate risk (S6), as well as the risk related to ineffective contingency plans (S7).

Company FS13 indicated that: "The consequence of the pandemic is an increase in the transactional risk arising from the situation in financial markets, which may adversely affect the appetite of financial institutions for building balance sheet exposures in the sector". Meanwhile, company FS17 emphasized that "The following risks associated with the pandemic were identified: the risk of interruption of services by some providers, the risk of slowing down processes due to reduced availability of external counterparties, the risk of reduced activity of market makers resulting in reduced liquidity of financial instruments" (FS17). The connection between the pandemic and environmental risks was also confirmed during the course of the research. For example, company FS25 noted that: "Thus, the daily work related to the lifting of the sanitary restrictions put in place due to the COVID-19 pandemic involves the consumption of office supplies, above all paper, electricity, heat, fuels".

- among business risks: the risk of changes in customers' behaviours and expectations (B4).

One company noted that: "In particular, what we observed during the pandemic was an increase in the importance of remote working and remote sales channels, as well as far-reaching changes in consumers' behaviours and needs for digital and mobile solutions" (FS23). Bank FS3 stressed that: "We plan to further "digitize" our sales and business model, taking advantage of the change in customers' preferences caused by the COVID-19 pandemic".

- among personnel risks: the risk of unhealthy or dangerous working conditions (P4), as well as the social risk (P6).

The examined enterprises emphasized that due to the pandemic, their catalogue of priority risks was extended to include: "The risk of periodic staff shortages due to the possibility of employees being infected by the virus or quarantined" (FS17). It was also confirmed by bank FS10: "We consider the pandemic and is impact on society as a new risk factor".

- among technological risks: the risk related to the digitization of operations (T3).

Some of the enterprises indicated that: "The pandemic and the associated restrictions contributed to the dynamic development of remote customer service processes ... A change that would normally take several years accelerated digitization, automation of processes and the use of advanced technologies" (FS23). Other enterprises also highlighted that: "The COVID-19 pandemic accelerated digital transformation" (FS10, FS4, FS1, FS9, FS23), and "User-friendly and secure digital operations and communications are now key to building competitive advantage" (FS10).

5.1.2   Construction sector

A comparison of the risk profiles of the examined enterprises representing the construction sector before and during the COVID-19 pandemic is presented graphically in Figure 5.2.

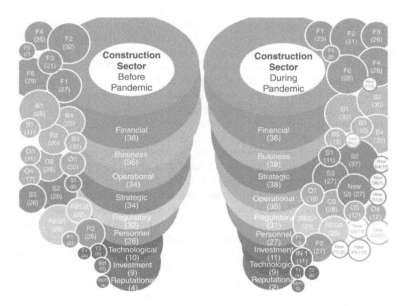

Figure 5.2 The risk profiles of the examined construction sector companies before and during the pandemic

Note: The results of the research on which the figure is based can be found in Appendix 5.2 at the end of this chapter.

Source: The authors' own work.

Compared to before the pandemic, the first change observed during its course concerned the exposure of the examined construction sector enterprises to individual risk factors. Analysing these developments with respect to the arrangement of risk categories, we observed subtle changes in the frequency of their identification. The most noticeable was the more frequent identification of strategic risks during the pandemic.

Conducting a more detailed analysis of the changes in risk exposure, i.e. with regard to specific risk factors from the respective categories, we noted more intensive changes caused by the pandemic in this sector. These changes concerned a marked increase in exposure to the price risk (F3), the supplier and subcontractor risk (B1), the financial result risk (B2), the risk of adverse changes in the sectoral market (B4), the macroeconomic risk (S2) and the legal risk (REG2). The most notable change occurred in exposure to the macroeconomic risk, with 28 enterprises identifying it before the pandemic and 37 ones during the pandemic. The examined enterprises declared experiencing the impact of the pandemic in their cooperation with stakeholders (including suppliers) in the form of: "shifts in performance schedules, problems with timely acceptance procedures, staff shortages" (CON6) "slowdowns in production cycles and delays in deliveries of equipment and materials due to transport restrictions or delays on the part of manufacturers/suppliers" (CON7). This, in turn, resulted in the intensification of the legal risk. The enterprises participating in the research mentioned the occurrence of: "Delays in obtaining administrative decisions and the fact that administrative decisions can be appealed" (CON3, CON12, CON21). Furthermore, "The effect of possible delays in the implementation of projects may result in disputes over the payment of remuneration for performed work, related in particular to the accrual of contractual penalties or damages by contractors for failure to perform contracts on time" (CON5). Also, the macroeconomic changes triggered by the pandemic had industry-specific consequences in the construction sector, e.g. those concerning "global supply chain problems caused by the tightened policy towards COVID-19" (CON26), and these, in turn, had measurable negative consequences for the bottom line of companies in the sector. The examined companies highlighted, for example, that: "Adverse developments related to the pandemic could lead to a downturn in the construction market, including through a lower supply of projects for general contractors, as well as cause a slowdown in growth and deterioration in profitability" (CON5, CON21). The price risk also become very important. Its increase was emphasized by a number of companies, including, for example, companies CON12 and CON27, which noted: "increases in commodity and material prices, contract administration costs and financial costs".

In the construction sector, new risks emerged during the pandemic that companies had not identified earlier. Brand new risks occurred in the following categories: financial (1), business (1), operational (2), strategic (4) and personnel (2). In total, we identified 10 new risks that occurred in the sector during the pandemic and were its direct or indirect consequences. Interestingly, during the pandemic a considerable majority of the examined enterprises (27 out of 38) started to experience pressure from a new risk related to the continuing COVID-19 pandemic (S5) and categorized it a strategic risk, emphasizing the key role of: "the uncertainty of the global economic situation, including risks related to the persisting pandemic" (CON3).

Other new risks that showed direct links to the impact of the pandemic were the following:

- among financial risks: the risk of diversification of funding sources (F7).

   For example, company CON8 indicated that: "it is essential for the business to maintain a sufficient level of external financing of assets, as well as the guarantee limits needed to hedge contracts. Excessively restrictive credit policies of banks and other financial institutions, due to the pandemic, may lead to a reduction in the required levels of financial limits (credit, guarantee, insurance, lease) in relation to the scale of operations".

- among business risks: the bankruptcy risk (B6).

   The examined companies began to realize that: "the economic crisis caused by the pandemic may affect the financial position of the company's business partners and cause delays in the payment of receivables or even total insolvency of those entities (CON5).

- among operational risks: the risk related to the size of the order book, weakening demand and changes in customers' expectations (O5), the risk of reduced availability of execution capacity and raw materials (O6).

   The examined companies perceived "the risk of the temporary closure of hotels during the pandemic. One could also mention the risk of a temporary reduction in demand for residential properties, which could result in fewer contracts being concluded for the sale of such properties" (CON5) and "major difficulties with the availability of raw materials and increases in their prices due to the ongoing pandemic" (CON10). Furthermore, "The continuing pandemic situation around the world and the consequent difficulties in the global supply chain resulted in wide fluctuations in the number of orders and production constraints, and the situation necessitated the diversification of sales destinations" (CON15).

- among strategic risks: the risk related to growth and expansion into new markets (S4), the risk related to the occurrence of unforeseeable events and their handling (S6), the risk related to failure to achieve strategic objectives (S7).

   Some enterprises stressed that: "The potential risk of construction work being halted or slowed down and logistical impediments occurring may cause delays in construction operations in the future, resulting in the inability to complete investment projects on time. The above, in turn, may increase the risk of potential buyers withdrawing from contracts already concluded" (CON5). According to the examined companies, the pandemic hampered the pursuit of strategic objectives "due to, among other things, the numerous restrictions caused by the pandemic, our strategic plans are being carried out with considerable delays" (CON19) and disrupted expansion and development because of "the temporary closure of foreign markets during the pandemic" (CON36).

• among personnel risks: the social risk (P3), the risk of employees becoming infected with COVID-19 (P4).

With respect to social risks, during the pandemic contacts with different stakeholder groups deteriorated considerably, as was indicated, for example, by company CON2: "The form of communication is selected according to the specific characteristics and needs of the stakeholders' group concerned and also taking into account the communication possibilities, which may be limited, for example, by the restrictions related to the COVID-19 pandemic". Staffing issues related to the COVID-19 outbreak also became evident, which was highlighted by the majority of the examined enterprises.

5.1.3   IT sector

A comparison of the risk profiles of the examined enterprises representing the IT sector before and during the COVID-19 pandemic is presented graphically in Figure 5.3.

Compared to before the pandemic, the first change observed during its course concerned the exposure of the examined IT sector companies to individual risk factors. Analysing these changes with respect to the arrangement of risk categories, we observed quite clear differences in the frequency of their identification., especially with regard to operational risks, which had been identified by 22 of the 41 examined companies before the pandemic, while during the pandemic they were identified by 27 of them. Exposure to investment risks also increased noticeably, from 21 of the 41 enterprises participating in the research monitoring such risk before the pandemic, to 25 of them doing this during the pandemic.

Conducting a more detailed analysis of the changes in risk exposure, i.e. with regard to specific risk factors from the respective categories, we noted considerable changes triggered by the pandemic. The most significant of them included a marked increase in exposure to the risk related to the process of winning new contracts and customers (B1), the financial result risk (B2), the risk of failure to achieve strategic goals (S1) and the ethical risk (P1). For example, company IT2 indicated that: "in view of the general slowdown in the economy resulting from the pandemic, the management perceives the

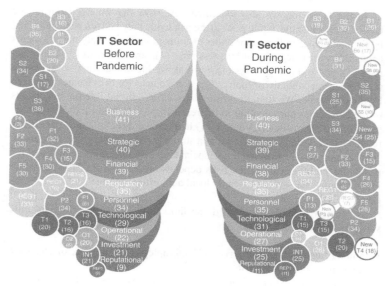

Figure 5.3 The risk profiles of the examined IT sector companies before and during the pandemic

Note: The results of the research on which the figure is based can be found in Appendix 5.3 at the end of this chapter.

Source: The authors' own work.

possibility of delays in settlements with customers, especially in the industries most affected by the pandemic". The direct impact of the pandemic on financial performance was highlighted by company IT20: "The issuer identified also other risks associated with the pandemic. They included the deterioration of the financial condition of the Group's customers, the emergence of payment bottlenecks in counterparties, the reduction or delay of IT investments by the Group's customers, delays in order fulfilment by suppliers, postponement of orders and delivery, as well as exchange rate volatility." Company IT5 confirmed the impact of the pandemic on the implementation of its strategy: "In 2021, the Group, in line with its development strategy, was taking proactive steps to realize its potential and market opportunities in pursuit of more dynamic growth. However, factors beyond the Issuer's control, namely the ongoing pandemic, the loss of industrial safety certificates and delays in product deliveries due to disruptions in the supply chain of the Company's key supplier, negatively impacted the results achieved and hindered the implementation of the strategy."

In the IT sector, we also identified new risks that emerged during the COVID-19 pandemic, while prior to the pandemic they had not been identified by the companies in the sector under examination. Completely new elements appeared in the categories of business risks (2), strategic risks (3), personnel risks (1), and technology risks (1). In total, we identified 7 new risks whose occurrence was directly or indirectly a consequence of the changes triggered by the pandemic. We found confirmations for this in the internal documents of the companies participating in the research project. During the pandemic, some of the enterprises (25 out of 41) had to face directly a new pandemic-related risk (S4) and categorized it as a strategic risk. As one enterprise stated: "Our companies are exposed to the social and economic consequences of the pandemic, and the scale of the risks depends on the course of the pandemic in the country, the actions taken by local authorities, and the profile of operations" (IT4).

Other new risks that showed direct links to the impact of the pandemic were the following:

- among business risks: the risk of bankruptcy (B5), the risk of changing customers' behaviours (B6).

    Changing customers' preferences and behaviours in the sector during the pandemic was indicated repeatedly by the examined enterprises. Company IT4 confirmed this as follows: "The pandemic triggered a significant acceleration in the growth of e-commerce transactions. In the opinion of the Management Board, the changed pattern of customers' behaviours is permanent and will not be reversed even after a possible relaxation of the restrictions related to the pandemic". Company IT6 indicated that: "Various businesses are taking advantage of the increasing interest in integrating digital content into learning processes caused by the Covid-19 pandemic and are preparing offers of dedicated products tailored to the specific needs of the different types of customers operating in the sector". The potential risk of bankruptcy also became a significant concern for some organizations: "As a result of the outbreak of the Covid-19 pandemic, the number of companies in Poland that declare bankruptcy has increased - this also applies to the contractors with whom the Group cooperates" (IT26).
- among the strategic risks: the environmental and climate risk (S5), the risk of natural disasters, catastrophes or emergencies (S6).

    For example, company IT9 indicated that: "The risk of catastrophic events and extraordinary risks, including epidemiological phenomena, can have a long-term impact on customers' behaviours or on the correct operation of the technical infrastructure of individual entities belonging to the Group or its customers." It turned out that the pandemic also had had an impact on environmental risks. This was confirmed, among others, by company IT26: "It should be noted, however, that for the outdoor advertising market, badly weakened by the effects of the COVID-19 pandemic, facing the requirements of various landscape resolutions may imply a periodic deterioration in performance during the transition period of the first years of new local regulations on outdoor advertising".

•   among personnel risks: the social risk (P3).

Company IT31 stressed that: "the pandemic conditions that accelerated the spread of remote working also caused greater acceptance of the "nearshoring" practice and the agile models of remote work. At the same time, there was quite significant upward pressure on the salaries of engineers and IT specialists."

•   among technological risks: risks related to digitization (T4).

The enterprises indicated a number of challenges related to pandemic-triggered digitization, greatly intensified due to the specific nature of the sector. For example, company IT3 highlighted additional costs generated by digitization processes: "Expenditure on IT will be driven by the wave of accelerated digital business transformation initiated by the COVID-19 crisis". The accelerated digital transformation process was also mentioned by other companies participating in the research, Company IT11 noted that: "The pandemic accelerated the digital transformation process. The recent quarters confirm that this is an irreversible process. As a result, more and more companies are adopting solutions such as LiveChat, Chat-Bot, KnowledgeBase or HelpDesk, which is confirmed by the still rapidly growing number of our customers". The problem of cybercrime was also mentioned in connection with digitization: "Ensuring data security and business continuity is becoming increasingly important, especially now, in consequence of the surge in cybercriminal activity during the coronavirus pandemic" (IT23).

5.2   The impact of the pandemic on modifications to the risk profiles of the analysed enterprises – An inter-sectoral comparison

According to our research, the COVID-19 pandemic influenced the introduction of modifications in the risk profiles of the enterprises participating in the research and representing the financial, construction and IT sectors. In order to present more vividly the changes in the risk profiles presented by sector in Section 5.1, we decided to present them in an arrangement based on risk categories. We started our analyses with a comparison of the lists of the risk categories identified by the examined companies as being of primary importance before the pandemic and during its course, respectively (Figure 5.4).

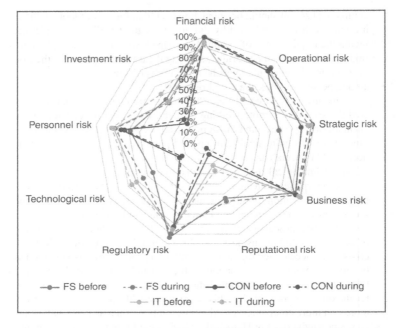

Figure 5.4 The percentage of FS, CON and IT enterprises identifying risks from the
particular categories before and during the pandemic – an inter-sectoral
comparison

Note: The results of the research on which the figure is based can be found in Appendices 5.1, 5.2
and 5.3 at the end of this chapter.

Source: The authors' own work.

As can be seen from the data in Figure 5.4, before the pandemic there were
significant differences in the prioritization of risks by the companies belonging to the three respective sectors. The differences were most noticeable in the
case of strategic, reputational, technological and operational risks, and were
largely determined by the specifics of each sector.

The research showed that strategic risks prior to the pandemic had been
the most frequently identified in the IT sector, with as many as 40 of the
41 examined companies (i.e. 98%) indicating them. The situation was quite
different in the case of the reputational risk. It turned out that this risk had
been the most often identified by companies from the financial sector; al-
though only 15 out of the 28 examined financial companies (54%) indicated
them, this result was the highest, as this type of risk had been identified by
only 11% of the companies from the construction sector and 22% of those

representing the IT sector. There were also notable differences between the three sectors with respect to technological risks. Risks in this category were identified the most often by the companies in the IT sector (29 out of the 41 participating companies, or 71%). Slightly less frequently, these risks were identified by the financial enterprises (15 out of the 28 enterprises, or 54%), and the least frequently the construction sector representatives (10 out of the 38 businesses, or 26%). On the other hand, analysing operational risks, we noticed that they had been indicated significantly less frequently by the companies in the IT sector than by those representing the other two sectors (only 22 out of the 41 enterprises, or 54%). In the case of the construction and financial sectors, risks in this category were identified by 89% of the companies.

During the COVID-19 pandemic, changes in the risk profiles between the companies belonging to the three sectors were also noticeable. We saw the greatest differences between the sectors during the pandemic in the case of the operational, reputational, technological and investment risk categories.

With regard to operational risks, the pre-pandemic trend was maintained and they were again identified the least frequently by the companies in the IT sector (27 out of the 41 companies, or 66%). In the case of technological risks, it is worth noting that their significance grew in the financial sector (during the pandemic, they were indicated by 18 out of the 28 participating enterprises, or 64%). For the IT sector, we also noted an increase in the importance of these risks, to the level of 76%. For the period of the pandemic, we also saw significant dissonance for risks in the investment category. They were the most frequently identified by the companies in the IT sector (61%), slightly less frequently by those in the financial sector (50%), and the least frequently by those in the construction sector (29%). Reputational risks were again the most frequently identified in the financial sector (57% of the companies), less frequently in the IT sector (27% of the companies), and the least frequently in the construction sector (5% of the companies).

Comparing the most characteristic modifications in the risk profiles of the examined companies from each sector during the pandemic to the period before its onset, we also noted a significant increase in the importance of strategic risks in the case of the financial and construction sectors. For the financial sector, this was an increase from 68% to 96%, while for the construction sector – from 89% to 100%.

Appendices

Appendix 5.1 The research results concerning the risk profile of financial sector enterprises before and during the pandemic

Risk category	Entities identifying risks in the particular categories before the pandemic	Total number	%	Entities identifying risks in the particular categories during the pandemic	Total number	%	Risk factors	Entities identifying a risk factor before the pandemic	Total	Entities identifying a risk factor during the pandemic	Total
FINANCIAL / CREDIT	1, 2, 3, 4, 5, 6, 7, 8, 9, 10, 11, 12, 13, 14, 15, 16, 17, 18, 19, 20, 21, 22, 23, 24, 25, 26, 27, 28	28	100	1, 2, 3, 4, 5, 6, 7, 8, 9, 10, 11, 12, 13, 14, 15, 16, 17, 19, 20, 21, 22, 23, 25, 26, 27, 28	26	93					
	1, 2, 3, 4, 5, 6, 7, 8, 9, 10, 11, 12, 13, 14, 15, 16, 17, 18, 20, 21, 22, 23, 24, 25, 26, 27, 28	27	96	1, 2, 3, 4, 5, 6, 7, 8, 9, 10, 11, 12, 13, 14, 15, 17, 20, 21, 22, 23, 26, 27, 28	23	82	C1 Concentration risk	1, 2, 4, 5, 6, 7, 9, 10, 11, 13, 14, 17, 20, 21, 23, 25, 26, 27, 28	19	1, 2, 4, 5, 6, 7, 8, 9, 11, 12, 13, 14, 17, 20, 21, 23, 26, 27, 28	19
							C2 Counterparty/customer risk	1, 2, 3, 4, 5, 6, 7, 8, 9, 10, 11, 12, 13, 14, 15, 16, 18, 20, 21, 22, 23, 24, 26, 27, 28	25	1, 2, 3, 4, 5, 6, 7, 8, 9, 10, 11, 12, 13, 14, 15, 20, 21, 22, 23, 26, 27, 28	22
							C3 Residual risk (concerning security)	1, 2, 3, 4, 5, 6, 7, 8, 9, 11, 12, 14, 21	13	1, 2, 5, 6, 9	5
							C4 Risk of credit valuation adjustments or unexpected changes in the borrower's creditworthiness		0	1, 2, 3, 4, 5, 9	6
							C5 Risk of forbearance practices		0	1, 12	2

	FINANCIAL											
	Risk	List			List			List		List	
MARKET	M1 Interest rate risk	1, 2, 3, 4, 5, 6, 7, 8, 9, 10, 11, 12, 13, 14, 15, 16, 17, 18, 19, 20, 21, 22, 23, 24, 26, 27	26	93	1, 2, 3, 4, 5, 6, 7, 8, 9, 10, 11, 12, 13, 14, 15, 17, 19, 20, 21, 22, 23, 27	23	82	1, 2, 3, 4, 5, 6, 7, 8, 9, 10, 11, 12, 13, 14, 15, 17, 18, 20, 21, 22, 23, 26, 27	23	1, 2, 3, 4, 5, 6, 7, 8, 9, 10, 11, 12, 13, 14, 15, 17, 20, 21, 22, 23, 27	21
	M2 Currency risk							1, 2, 3, 4, 5, 6, 7, 8, 9, 10, 11, 12, 13, 14, 15, 16, 19, 20, 21, 22, 23, 24, 27	23	1, 2, 3, 4, 5, 6, 7, 8, 9, 10, 11, 12, 14, 15, 16, 19, 20, 21, 22, 23, 27	21
	M3 Price risk							1, 2, 5, 6, 7, 12, 13, 21, 22, 23, 26	11	1, 2, 3, 4, 5, 9, 10, 12, 14, 17, 21, 22, 23, 27	14
LIQUIDITY	L1 Financial liquidity risk (risk of failure to meet financial obligations due to customers and counterparties)	1, 2, 3, 4, 5, 6, 7, 8, 9, 10, 11, 12, 13, 14, 15, 18, 20, 21, 22, 26, 27	21	75	1, 2, 3, 4, 5, 6, 7, 8, 9, 10, 11, 12, 13, 14, 15, 17, 20, 21, 22, 23, 25, 26, 27	23	82	1, 2, 4, 5, 6, 7, 8, 9, 10, 11, 12, 13, 14, 15, 18, 20, 21, 22, 26, 27	20	1, 2, 3, 4, 5, 6, 7, 8, 9, 10, 11, 12, 13, 14, 15, 17, 20, 21, 22, 23, 25, 27	22
	L2 Risk of excessive leverage (risk of excessive growth of credit exposure relative to equity that may cause liquidity problems or losses)							3, 4, 5, 6, 9, 11, 12	7	1, 3, 5, 6, 8, 9, 12	7
	L3 Excessive indebtedness/insolvency risk								0	3, 6, 10, 12, 26, 27	6
INSURANCE	I1 Risk related to insurance activities, offering of insurance products or insufficient insurance cover		0	0	2, 5, 11, 17, 23	5	18		0	2, 5, 11, 17, 23	5

(Continued)

Appendix 5.1 (Continued)

Risk category	Entities identifying risks in the particular categories before the pandemic	Total number	%	Entities identifying risks in the particular categories during the pandemic	Total number	%	Risk factors	Entities identifying a risk factor before the pandemic	Total	Entities identifying a risk factor during the pandemic	Total
OPERATIONAL	1, 2, 3, 4, 5, 6, 7, 8, 9, 10, 11, 12, 13, 14, 15, 16, 17, 18, 19, 21, 23, 25, 26, 27, 28	25	89	1, 2, 3, 4, 5, 7, 8, 9, 10, 11, 12, 13, 15, 16, 17, 18, 19, 20, 21, 22, 23, 24, 25, 26, 27, 28	26	93	O1 Risk of loss due to inadequate or error-prone internal processes, operational errors, systems or external events	1, 2, 3, 4, 5, 6, 7, 8, 9, 10, 11, 12, 13, 14, 17, 21, 23, 27, 28	19	1, 2, 3, 4, 5, 7, 8, 9, 10, 11, 12, 13, 17, 18, 23, 24, 25, 27, 28	19
							O2 Outsourcing risk (which may result in a negative impact on business continuity, integrity, stability or quality)	2, 5, 11, 14	4	1, 2, 6, 11	4
							O3 Product risk (risk associated with distribution channels or with the entity's sale of products (services) that do not meet customers' requirements and needs, generate additional risks (for the entity and its customers), lack adequate staff support and processes	1, 2, 3, 5, 6, 7, 8, 14, 15, 16, 18, 19, 23, 25, 26, 27, 28	17	1, 2, 3, 4, 10, 15, 16, 18, 19, 21, 23, 24, 25, 26, 27, 28	16
							O4 Risk of money laundering and terrorism financing – the risk of incurring losses as a result of being involved in money laundering and terrorism financing activities carried out by customers, intermediaries or employees		0	2, 3, 10, 25	4
							O5 Tax and accounting risk – the risk of negative economic consequences due to inadequate (incorrect) accounting records and reporting, miscalculation of tax liabilities or failure to pay them on time		0	2, 16, 17, 20, 22	5
							O6 Customer complaints risk		0	10	1

Category		19	68	27	96	Risk		11		15
STRATEGIC		5, 6, 7, 8, 9, 11, 13, 14, 15, 16, 17, 18, 19, 21, 22, 24, 26, 27, 28	1, 2, 3, 4, 5, 6, 7, 8, 9, 10, 11, 12, 13, 14, 15, 16, 17, 18, 19, 20, 22, 23, 24, 25, 26, 27, 28	27	96	S1 Risk of incurring losses due to decisions or radical changes in the business environment, inadequate implementation of decisions/strategies, failure to respond to changes in the environment, e.g. a change in the trend of the economic cycle negatively affecting strategy implementation, changes in a strategy or strategic goals		5, 11, 14, 15, 17, 21, 22, 24, 26, 27, 28	11	2, 3, 4, 5, 6, 7, 8, 13, 15, 16, 17, 20, 22, 27, 28
						S2 Risk of changes in macroeconomic conditions (macroprudential risk) – the risk of changes in the macroeconomic environment that may affect future capital requirements or the level of equity		5, 6, 7, 8, 9, 11, 13, 14, 15, 16, 17, 18, 19, 22, 27	15	1, 3, 4, 5, 6, 7, 8, 9, 11, 15, 16, 17, 18, 19, 20, 22, 26, 27	18
						S3 Competition risk		15, 16, 17, 18, 19, 21, 22, 24, 26, 27	10	3, 15, 16, 17, 18, 19, 22, 26, 27	9
						S4 Institutional risk			0	1, 2, 7, 9, 13, 18	6
						S5 Risk of collaboration/transactions with or dependence on other entities, stakeholders (e.g. suppliers, shareholders, counterparties)			0	1, 7, 13, 16, 17, 18, 22, 23, 24, 25, 26, 27	12
						S6 Environmental and climate risk (e.g. related to penalties for non-compliance with environmental regulations, consumption of utilities, consumption and recycling of paper, reduction and replacement of vehicle fleets)			0	1, 2, 4, 5, 6, 9, 10, 17, 25	9
						S7 Risk related to stress conditions and ineffectiveness of contingency plans			0	6, 9, 10, 11, 12	5
						S8 Pandemic-related risk			0	3, 4, 7, 10, 12, 13, 14, 17, 18, 20, 23, 24, 27	13

(Continued)

Appendix 5.1 (Continued)

Risk category	Entities identifying risks in the particular categories before the pandemic	Total number	Total %	Entities identifying risks in the particular categories during the pandemic	Total number	Total %	Risk factors	Entities identifying a risk factor before the pandemic	Total	Entities identifying a risk factor during the pandemic	Total
BUSINESS	1, 2, 3, 4, 5, 6, 7, 8, 9, 10, 11, 12, 13, 14, 15, 16, 17, 18, 20, 21, 22, 24, 25, 26, 27, 28	26	93	1, 2, 3, 4, 5, 6, 7, 8, 9, 10, 11, 12, 13, 14, 15, 16, 17, 18, 20, 21, 22, 23, 24, 25, 26, 27, 28	27	96	B1 Model risk (potential losses that the entity may suffer as a result of business decisions based on data obtained through the use of models – due to errors in the development, implementation or application of such models)	1, 2, 3, 4, 5, 6, 8, 9, 10, 11, 12	11	1, 2, 5, 6, 9, 10, 11, 12, 23	9
							B2 Financial result risk (the risk of adverse, unexpected changes in capital, changes in operating costs, changes in business volumes and/or margins that are not due to credit, market or operational risks, but have an impact on financial performance and business continuity)	5, 6, 7, 9, 10, 11, 12, 13, 14, 15, 16, 17, 18, 20, 21, 22, 24, 25, 26, 27, 28	21	1, 2, 3, 4, 5, 6, 7, 8, 9, 11, 12, 13, 14, 15, 16, 17, 18, 20, 21, 22, 23, 24, 25, 26, 27, 28	26
							B3 Risk of losing key customers	16, 17, 21	3	16, 18, 21, 27	4
							B4 Risk of changing customers' behaviours and expectations		0	3, 4, 7, 9, 10, 13, 16, 18, 21, 23, 24, 27	12
REPUTATIONAL	1, 2, 5, 6, 7, 8, 10, 13, 14, 16, 17, 22, 25, 27, 28	15	54	1, 2, 4, 5, 6, 7, 8, 10, 13, 16, 17, 22, 25, 27, 28	16	57	REP 1 Reputational risk (the risk to revenue and capital arising from the negative perception of the financial institution by its customers, counterparties, shareholders, investors, regulators)	1, 2, 5, 6, 7, 8, 10, 13, 14, 16, 17, 22, 25, 27, 28	15	1, 2, 4, 5, 6, 7, 8, 10, 11, 13, 16, 17, 22, 25, 27, 28	16

Category							Risk				
REGULATORY	26	1, 2, 3, 4, 5, 7, 8, 9, 10, 11, 12, 13, 14, 15, 16, 17, 18, 19, 20, 21, 22, 23, 24, 25, 26, 27	93	1, 2, 3, 4, 5, 6, 7, 8, 9, 10, 11, 12, 13, 15, 16, 17, 18, 19, 20, 22, 23, 24, 25, 26, 27	25	89	REG 1 Non-compliance/sanction risk (the risk of legal or supervisory sanctions as a result of failure to comply with laws, regulators' recommendations, internal regulations and accepted standards of conduct)	1, 2, 3, 4, 5, 6, 7, 8, 9, 10, 11, 12, 13, 14, 15, 16, 17, 18, 19, 20, 21, 22, 23, 24, 25, 26, 27	27	1, 2, 3, 4, 5, 6, 7, 8, 9, 10, 11, 12, 13, 15, 16, 17, 18, 19, 20, 22, 23, 24, 25, 26, 27	25
							REG 2 Legal risk (the risk of incurring losses due to instability of legal regulations, changes in judicial decisions, erroneous formulation of legal relations, quality of formal and legal documentation or unfavourable decisions of courts or other authorities in disputes with other entities)	2, 6, 10, 12, 13, 14, 15, 16, 17, 18, 21, 22, 24, 25, 27	15	1, 2, 3, 4, 6, 7, 8, 9, 10, 12, 13, 15, 16, 17, 18, 20, 22, 23, 24, 25, 26, 27	22
TECHNOLOGICAL	15	2, 7, 8, 12, 14, 15, 17, 18, 21, 22, 24, 25, 26, 27, 28	54	1, 2, 3, 4, 6, 9, 10, 15, 17, 18, 21, 22, 23, 24, 25, 26, 27, 28	18	64	T1 Information, transaction and intellectual property rights security risk (including the cyber security risk)	2, 17, 21, 22, 24, 25, 26, 27	8	1, 2, 3, 6, 9, 10, 17, 22, 23, 24, 25, 26, 27	13
							T2 Business disruption risk due to failure in the functioning of information and communication systems	2, 7, 8, 12, 14, 15, 17, 18, 21, 22, 27, 28	12	1, 2, 3, 6, 9, 15, 17, 18, 21, 22, 24, 28	12
							T3 Risk related to the digitization of the entity's own business/digital transformation and the digitization of its business partners		0	1, 2, 3, 4, 9, 10, 17, 23, 25, 27	10

(Continued)

Appendix 5.1 (Continued)

Risk category	Entities identifying risks in the particular categories before the pandemic	Total number	%	Entities identifying risks in the particular categories during the pandemic	Total number	%	Risk factors	Entities identifying a risk factor before the pandemic	Total	Entities identifying a risk factor during the pandemic	Total
PERSONNEL	1, 2, 3, 7, 8, 11, 13, 14, 15, 16, 17, 18, 19, 21, 22, 24, 25, 27, 28	19	68	1, 2, 3, 5, 6, 7, 9, 10, 11, 13, 15, 16, 17, 18, 19, 20, 21, 22, 23, 24, 25, 27, 28	23	82	P1 Risk of fraud/embezzlement/corruption (the risk of deliberate harm caused by employees or third parties)	2, 3, 7, 8, 14, 18, 21	7	1, 2, 3, 10, 17, 22, 27	7
							P2 Personnel risk (the risk related to recruitment, availability and professional qualifications of employees, their turnover, adaptability to the work environment, work culture, absenteeism, nepotism)	1, 2, 7, 8, 13, 14, 15, 16, 17, 18, 19, 21, 22, 24, 25, 27, 28	17	1, 2, 3, 9, 13, 15, 16, 17, 18, 19, 21, 22, 24, 25, 28	15
							P3 Misconduct risk (the risk of employees' or intermediaries' intentionally or negligently causing harm to customers, the integrity of financial markets or the integrity of the entity)	1, 2, 7, 8, 11, 14, 18	7	1, 2, 11, 17, 18, 24, 25, 27	8
							P4 Risk of unhealthy or dangerous working conditions		0	3, 7, 10, 27	4
							P5 Ethical risk – the risk of non-compliance with ethical principles and human rights		0	2, 3, 9, 10, 22, 24, 25, 27	8
							P6 Social risk		0	2, 5, 6, 9, 10, 20, 23, 25	8

INVESTMENT		15	54		14	50			15		14
	1, 3, 5, 10, 14, 15, 16, 17, 18, 19, 20, 21, 22, 25, 27			1, 4, 5, 9, 10, 15, 16, 17, 18, 19, 20, 23, 25, 27			IN1 Capital market business cycle risk /capital risk (the risk of unexpected adverse changes in the value of capital invested in stocks or shares or the risk arising from adverse changes in the shareholding structure)	1, 3, 5, 10, 14, 15, 16, 17, 18, 19, 20, 21, 22, 25, 27		1, 4, 5, 9, 10, 15, 16, 17, 18, 19, 20, 23, 25, 27	
							IN2 Real property risk – the risk of losses resulting from market fluctuations in the value of a real property portfolio		0	5, 26	2

Source: The authors' own work.

Appendix 5.2 The research results concerning the risk profile of construction sector enterprises before and during the pandemic

Risk category	Entities identifying risks in the particular categories before the pandemic	Total		Entities identifying risks in the particular categories during the pandemic	Total		Risk factors	Entities identifying a risk factor before the pandemic	Total	Entities identifying a risk factor during the pandemic	Total
		number	%		number	%					
FINANCIAL	1, 2, 3, 4, 5, 6, 7, 8, 9, 10, 11, 12, 13, 14, 15, 16, 17, 18, 19, 20, 21, 22, 23, 24, 25, 26, 27, 28, 29, 30, 31, 32, 33, 34, 35, 36, 37, 38	38	100	1, 2, 3, 4, 5, 6, 7, 8, 9, 10, 11, 12, 13, 14, 15, 16, 17, 18, 19, 20, 21, 22, 23, 24, 25, 26, 27, 28, 29, 30, 31, 32, 33, 34, 35, 36, 37, 38	38	100	F1 Interest rate risk	1, 3, 4, 5, 8, 9, 10, 15, 16, 17, 18, 20, 21, 22, 24, 25, 27, 28, 29, 30, 31, 32, 33, 35, 36, 37, 38	27	1, 3, 4, 5, 8, 9, 10, 13, 15, 16, 17, 18, 20, 21, 24, 25, 26, 27, 29, 30, 31, 32, 33, 36, 38	25
							F2 Currency risk	2, 4, 5, 6, 7, 8, 9, 10, 11, 12, 14, 15, 16, 17, 18, 20, 21, 23, 24, 25, 26, 27, 28, 29, 30, 31, 32, 33, 35, 36, 37, 38	32	1, 2, 4, 5, 7, 8, 9, 10, 11, 12, 13, 14, 15, 16, 17, 18, 20, 21, 23, 24, 25, 27, 28, 29, 30, 31, 32, 33, 35, 36, 37	31
							F3 Price risk	1, 2, 3, 7, 9, 14, 15, 16, 19, 20, 22, 23, 25, 27, 29, 30, 31, 33, 36, 37, 38	21	1, 2, 3, 5, 6, 7, 8, 9, 11, 12, 13, 15, 16, 17, 19, 20, 22, 23, 25, 27, 29, 30, 31, 32, 36, 37	26

Category	Risk	n	Respondents	n	Respondents
FINANCIAL	F4 Liquidity risk	25	1, 2, 3, 4, 9, 10, 11, 16, 17, 19, 22, 23, 24, 25, 27, 28, 29, 31, 32, 33, 34, 35, 36, 37, 38	28	1, 2, 3, 4, 5, 6, 8, 9, 10, 12, 13, 16, 17, 19, 21, 24, 25, 26, 27, 29, 30, 31, 32, 33, 34, 36, 37, 38
	F5 Insurance risk (insufficient insurance cover for contracts, property, persons)	7	1, 9, 22, 24, 27, 30, 33	8	1, 2, 8, 24, 25, 27, 30, 32
	F6 Credit risk (relating to creditworthiness of the entity, as well as its counterparties, investors, customers)	29	1, 2, 3, 4, 5, 8, 9, 13, 15, 16, 17, 20, 21, 22, 23, 24, 25, 27, 28, 29, 30, 31, 32, 33, 34, 35, 36, 37, 38	28	3, 4, 5, 8, 10, 11, 12, 13, 15, 16, 17, 18, 19, 20, 21, 23, 24, 25, 26, 27, 29, 30, 31, 32, 33, 34, 36, 37
	F7 Risk of diversification of financing sources and cooperation with financial institutions	0		3	5, 8, 30

(Continued)

Appendix 5.2 (Continued)

Risk category	Entities identifying risks in the particular categories before the pandemic	Total number	%	Entities identifying risks in the particular categories during the pandemic	Total number	%	Risk factors	Entities identifying a risk factor before the pandemic	Total	Entities identifying a risk factor during the pandemic	Total
OPERATIONAL	1, 2, 3, 4, 5, 6, 7, 8, 9, 10, 11, 12, 13, 14, 15, 17, 18, 19, 21, 22, 23, 24, 25, 26, 27, 28, 29, 30, 32, 33, 34, 36, 37, 38	34	89	1, 2, 3, 4, 5, 6, 7, 8, 9, 10, 11, 12, 13, 15, 16, 17, 18, 19, 21, 22, 23, 24, 25, 26, 27, 28, 29, 30, 32, 33, 34, 35, 36, 37, 38	35	92	O1 Technical and operational risk (including the risk related to technical infrastructure, machinery, breakdowns, wear and tear of equipment, loss of fixed assets, product defects)	1, 3, 4, 8, 10, 11, 12, 13, 15, 19, 21, 23, 24, 25, 27, 30, 32, 34, 36, 37	20	1, 5, 9, 10, 11, 12, 13, 15, 17, 21, 24, 27, 28, 30, 32, 35, 36, 37	18
							O2 Contract risk (the risk of seeking, obtaining, failing to fulfil or improperly fulfilling the terms of agreements/contracts/tenders)	1, 2, 3, 5, 6, 7, 8, 9, 10, 12, 13, 19, 21, 22, 23, 24, 25, 26, 27, 28, 29, 30, 32, 33, 34, 36, 37, 38	28	1, 2, 3, 5, 6, 7, 8, 9, 11, 12, 13, 16, 21, 22, 23, 24, 25, 26, 27, 28, 29, 30, 32, 33, 34, 36, 37, 38	28
							O3 Risk of occupational safety, including the occurrence of accidents at work	1, 2, 5, 6, 13, 19, 23, 24, 25, 27, 30	11	1, 2, 5, 6, 10, 13, 17, 24, 27, 30, 35, 36	12
							O4 Environmental and climate risk (the risk of negative impact on the local community, environment and biodiversity, and the risk of adverse weather conditions and natural disasters)	2, 5, 6, 9, 10, 13, 14, 17, 18, 19, 21, 23, 24, 25, 27, 36, 38	17	2, 4, 6, 8, 9, 10, 16, 17, 18, 21, 24, 27, 30, 32, 33, 36, 38	17
							O5 Risk related to the size of the order book, the weakening of demand and changes in customers' expectations		0	1, 2, 3, 4, 5, 6, 8, 9, 10, 11, 13, 15, 21, 23, 25, 26, 28, 30, 32, 36, 37	21
							O6 Risk of reduced availability of execution capacity and raw materials necessary for contract performance		0	3, 4, 5, 6, 8, 10, 11, 16, 19, 25, 27, 32, 33, 37	14

The following table (continued from the previous page) concerns STRATEGIC risks.

Risk	Col (100)	Col (38)	Items (38)	Col (89)	Items (89)	Col (34)	Items (34)
S1 Risk related to the sector's seasonality	100	38	1, 2, 3, 4, 5, 6, 7, 8, 9, 10, 11, 12, 13, 14, 15, 16, 17, 18, 19, 20, 21, 22, 23, 24, 25, 26, 27, 28, 29, 30, 31, 32, 33, 34, 35, 36, 37, 38	89	1, 2, 3, 4, 5, 6, 7, 8, 9, 10, 11, 12, 13, 14, 15, 16, 17, 18, 19, 20, 21, 22, 23, 24, 25, 26, 27, 28, 29, 30, 31, 32, 33, 34, 35, 36, 37, 38	34	1, 3, 4, 5, 6, 7, 8, 9, 10, 11, 12, 14, 15, 16, 17, 18, 19, 20, 21, 22, 23, 24, 25, 26, 27, 29, 30, 31, 32, 33, 35, 36, 37, 38

Risk	Count	Items	Count	Items
S1 Risk related to the sector's seasonality	8	1, 7, 12, 14, 18, 20, 24, 32	11	1, 5, 7, 12, 14, 16, 18, 20, 24, 26, 32
S2 Macroeconomic risk (related to the state of the economy in Poland and Europe)	28	1, 3, 4, 5, 6, 7, 8, 9, 10, 11, 12, 14, 15, 16, 17, 18, 19, 21, 24, 25, 26, 27, 30, 31, 32, 36, 37, 38	37	1, 2, 3, 4, 5, 6, 7, 8, 9, 10, 11, 12, 13, 14, 15, 16, 17, 18, 19, 20, 21, 22, 23, 24, 25, 26, 27, 28, 30, 31, 32, 33, 34, 35, 36, 37, 38
S3 Competition risk	26	1, 4, 5, 7, 10, 11, 12, 14, 17, 18, 19, 20, 21, 22, 23, 24, 25, 27, 29, 30, 31, 32, 33, 35, 36, 38	27	1, 4, 5, 7, 8, 11, 12, 13, 14, 16, 17, 18, 20, 21, 22, 23, 24, 25, 27, 29, 31, 32, 33, 35, 36, 37, 38
S4 Risk related to development and expansion into new markets, including foreign markets	0		10	2, 8, 11, 12, 19, 26, 27, 35, 36, 37
S5 Risk related to the persisting COVID-19 pandemic	0		27	3, 4, 5, 6, 7, 8, 9, 10, 11, 12, 13, 14, 15, 16, 17, 18, 20, 21, 23, 25, 26, 30, 32, 33, 34, 36, 38
S6 Risk related to the occurrence of unforeseeable events and their handling	0		7	14, 15, 17, 27, 34, 36, 37
S7 Risk of failure to achieve strategic objectives	0		6	17, 20, 21, 25, 27, 36

STRATEGIC

(Continued)

Appendix 5.2 (Continued)

Risk category	Entities identifying risks in the particular categories before the pandemic	Total number	%	Entities identifying risks in the particular categories during the pandemic	Total number	%	Risk factors	Entities identifying a risk factor before the pandemic	Total	Entities identifying a risk factor during the pandemic	Total
BUSINESS	1, 2, 4, 5, 6, 8, 9, 10, 11, 12, 13, 14, 15, 16, 17, 18, 19, 20, 21, 22, 23, 24, 25, 26, 27, 28, 29, 30, 31, 32, 33, 34, 35, 36, 37, 38	36	95	1, 2, 3, 4, 5, 6, 7, 8, 9, 10, 11, 12, 13, 14, 15, 16, 17, 18, 19, 20, 21, 22, 23, 24, 25, 26, 27, 28, 29, 30, 31, 32, 33, 34, 35, 36, 37, 38	38	100	B1 Risk related to suppliers of materials and subcontractors, including supply chain risk (which may translate into a reduction in the quality of fulfilled orders and notable financial losses)	1, 2, 4, 5, 6, 8, 9, 10, 11, 12, 13, 15, 17, 18, 19, 22, 23, 24, 25, 26, 27, 29, 30, 31, 32, 33, 36, 38	28	1, 2, 3, 5, 6, 8, 9, 10, 11, 12, 13, 14, 15, 16, 17, 18, 19, 20, 21, 22, 23, 24, 25, 26, 29, 30, 31, 32, 33, 36, 37, 38	32
							B2 Financial result risk (the risk of changes in operating costs, insolvency of customers, employment costs, underestimated costs of contracts) affecting the financial result and business continuity	1, 2, 3, 5, 6, 8, 10, 11, 12, 13, 14, 17, 19, 20, 22, 24, 26, 27, 28, 29, 30, 32, 33, 35, 36, 38	26	1, 2, 3, 5, 6, 7, 8, 9, 11, 12, 13, 14, 15, 16, 17, 18, 19, 20, 24, 25, 26, 27, 29, 30, 32, 33, 34, 36, 37, 38	30
							B3 Risk of dependence on key customers	1, 5, 10, 12, 17, 18, 24, 26, 28, 32, 33, 36	12	1, 12, 24, 26, 30, 18, 28, 32, 33, 36	10
							B4 Risk of changes in the sectoral market (the risk related to changes in prevailing sectoral trends, distribution channels and mismatches between the product mix and the market)	4, 5, 6, 9, 10, 11, 12, 15, 16, 17, 18, 19, 21, 24, 25, 26, 27, 28, 31, 32, 34, 35, 36, 37, 38	25	2, 3, 4, 5, 6, 8, 11, 12, 14, 15, 16, 17, 18, 19, 20, 21, 23, 24, 25, 26, 27, 28, 31, 32, 33, 34, 35, 36, 37	29
							B5 Risk of deteriorating relations with business partners or business partners' unreliability	2, 8, 12, 13, 19, 20, 23, 25, 26, 29, 36	11	11, 12, 17, 20, 25, 26, 27, 29, 30, 32, 36, 37, 38	13
							B6 Bankruptcy risk		0	30, 38	2

REPUTATIONAL	1, 2, 13, 30	4	11	10, 30	2	5	REP 1 Reputational risk (the risk to revenue arising from the negative perception of the entity by its customers, counterparties, shareholders, investors and potential business partners, as well as marketing communication failures)	1, 2, 13, 30	4	10, 30	2
REGULATORY	1, 2, 3, 4, 5, 6, 7, 8, 9, 10, 11, 12, 13, 14, 15, 17, 18, 19, 21, 23, 24, 25, 26, 27, 29, 30, 31, 32, 33, 35, 36, 38	32	84	1, 2, 3, 4, 5, 6, 7, 8, 9, 10, 11, 12, 13, 14, 15, 16, 17, 18, 21, 23, 24, 25, 26, 27, 29, 30, 31, 32, 33, 36, 38	31	82	REG 1 Non-compliance risk (the risk of legal sanctions as a result of failure to comply with changes in construction, tax, environmental protection, public procurement, concessions, and sectoral regulations, as well as internal regulations and accepted standards of conduct)	1, 2, 3, 4, 5, 6, 8, 9, 10, 11, 12, 13, 14, 15, 17, 18, 19, 21, 23, 24, 25, 26, 27, 29, 30, 31, 32, 33, 36, 38	30	1, 2, 3, 4, 5, 6, 8, 9, 10, 11, 12, 13, 14, 15, 16, 17, 18, 21, 24, 25, 26, 27, 29, 30, 31, 32, 33, 36, 38	29
							REG 2 Legal risk (the risk of incurring losses due to unfavourable formation of legal relations, unfavourable administrative decisions, unfavourable decisions of courts or other authorities in disputes with other entities and the need to pay contractual penalties and damages)	1, 2, 3, 5, 6, 7, 9, 12, 13, 17, 21, 23, 24, 25, 26, 27, 30, 32, 33, 35, 36, 38	22	1, 2, 3, 4, 5, 6, 7, 8, 9, 11, 12, 13, 14, 17, 21, 23, 24, 25, 26, 27, 30, 32, 33, 36, 38	25
TECHNOLOGICAL	2, 6, 8, 10, 11, 13, 23, 24, 30, 36	10	26	2, 5, 6, 9, 13, 24, 30, 34, 36	9	24	T1 Information security risk (including cybercrime risk)	6, 10, 13, 30	4	2, 6, 9, 30	4
							T2 Information technology risk (the risk related to the use of information systems and modern technologies supporting order fulfilment)	2, 8, 10, 11, 23, 24, 30, 36	8	2, 5, 9, 13, 24, 30, 34, 36	8

(Continued)

Appendix 5.2 (Continued)

Risk category	Entities identifying risks in the particular categories before the pandemic	Total number	%	Entities identifying risks in the particular categories during the pandemic	Total number	%	Risk factors	Entities identifying a risk factor before the pandemic	Total	Entities identifying a risk factor during the pandemic	Total
PERSONNEL	1, 2, 3, 4, 5, 6, 8, 9, 10, 11, 12, 13, 17, 19, 20, 23, 24, 25, 27, 28, 29, 30, 32, 33, 34, 36, 37, 38	28	74	1, 2, 3, 4, 5, 6, 8, 9, 10, 11, 12, 13, 16, 17, 19, 20, 21, 24, 25, 26, 27, 28, 29, 30, 32, 33, 36, 37, 38	27	71	P1 Ethical risk (the risk of employees' or third parties' unethical behaviours, including corruption, to the detriment of the entity)	2, 5, 11, 13, 19, 25, 27, 38	8	2, 10, 38	3
							P2 Personnel risk (the risk related to recruitment, availability and professional qualifications of employees, their turnover, adaptability to the work environment, work culture, absenteeism)	1, 2, 3, 4, 6, 8, 9, 10, 12, 13, 17, 19, 20, 23, 24, 25, 27, 28, 29, 30, 32, 33, 34, 36, 37, 38	26	1, 3, 4, 5, 6, 8, 9, 10, 12, 13, 16, 17, 19, 20, 21, 24, 25, 26, 27, 28, 29, 30, 32, 33, 36, 37, 38	27
							P3 Social risk		0	2, 9, 10, 36, 38	5
							P4 Risk of employees becoming infected with COVID-19		0	3, 8, 10, 11, 12, 16, 21, 27, 30, 32, 37, 38	12
INVESTMENT	5, 7, 8, 12, 17, 23, 29, 31, 32	9	24	5, 6, 7, 12, 17, 27, 28, 29, 30, 31, 32	11	29	IN 1 Capital market business cycle risk (the risk of unexpected adverse changes in the value of capital invested in stocks or shares, the risk of issuing the entity's own securities or the risk arising from adverse changes in the shareholding structure)	5, 7, 8, 12, 17, 23, 29, 31, 32	9	5, 6, 7, 12, 17, 27, 28, 29, 30, 31, 32	11

Source: The authors' own work.

Appendix 5.3 The research results concerning the risk profile of IT sector enterprises before and during the pandemic

Risk category	Entities identifying risks in the particular categories before the pandemic	Total number	%	Entities identifying risks in the particular categories during the pandemic	Total number	%	Risk factors	Entities identifying a risk factor before the pandemic	Total	Entities identifying a risk factor during the pandemic	Total
FINANCIAL	1, 2, 3, 4, 5, 6, 7, 8, 9, 10, 11, 12, 13, 14, 16, 17, 18, 19, 20, 22, 23, 24, 25, 26, 27, 28, 29, 30, 31, 32, 33, 34, 35, 36, 37, 38, 39, 40, 41	39	95	1, 3, 4, 5, 6, 7, 8, 9, 10, 11, 12, 13, 14, 16, 17, 18, 19, 20, 21, 22, 23, 24, 25, 26, 27, 28, 29, 30, 32, 33, 34, 35, 36, 37, 38, 39, 40, 41	38	93	F1 Interest rate risk	1, 2, 3, 4, 5, 6, 7, 8, 12, 13, 14, 16, 17, 18, 19, 22, 23, 24, 25, 26, 27, 28, 29, 30, 31, 32, 35, 36, 37, 39, 40, 41	32	1, 3, 4, 5, 6, 7, 8, 12, 16, 17, 21, 22, 23, 24, 25, 26, 27, 29, 30, 32, 34, 35, 36, 38, 39, 40, 41	27
							F2 Currency risk	1, 2, 3, 4, 5, 6, 7, 8, 9, 10, 11, 12, 13, 14, 16, 17, 18, 20, 22, 24, 25, 26, 28, 29, 30, 31, 32, 33, 35, 36, 39, 40, 41	33	1, 3, 4, 5, 6, 7, 8, 9, 10, 11, 12, 13, 14, 16, 17, 18, 20, 21, 22, 24, 25, 26, 27, 29, 30, 32, 33, 35, 36, 38, 39, 40, 41	33
							F3 Price risk	1, 8, 10, 12, 14, 16, 19, 23, 25, 27, 28, 32, 34, 37, 41	15	1, 6, 8, 10, 11, 14, 16, 19, 23, 26, 27, 32, 36, 37, 41	15
							F4 Liquidity risk	1, 2, 3, 4, 5, 7, 8, 9, 10, 12, 13, 14, 16, 17, 19, 22, 23, 24, 25, 26, 28, 29, 30, 31, 32, 35, 36, 37, 40, 41	30	1, 4, 5, 7, 8, 9, 10, 11, 12, 16, 19, 22, 23, 24, 26, 27, 29, 30, 32, 34, 35, 36, 37, 38, 39, 40	26

(Continued)

Appendix 5.3 (Continued)

64   *Impact of the COVID-19 pandemic*

Risk category	Entities identifying risks in the particular categories before the pandemic	Total number	%	Entities identifying risks in the particular categories during the pandemic	Total number	%	Risk factors	Entities identifying a risk factor before the pandemic	Total	Entities identifying a risk factor during the pandemic	Total
FINANCIAL	2, 3, 4, 5, 6, 7, 9, 14, 17, 18, 19, 20, 21, 23, 28, 29, 32, 33, 35, 38, 39, 40	22	54	1, 2, 3, 4, 5, 6, 7, 9, 12, 13, 14, 17, 18, 19, 20, 21, 23, 29, 30, 32, 33, 34, 35, 38, 39, 40, 41	27	66	F5 Credit risk (the risk related to securing additional sources of funding and the risk of business partners' creditworthiness)	1, 2, 3, 5, 6, 7, 8, 10, 12, 13, 14, 16, 17, 19, 20, 22, 24, 25, 27, 28, 29, 30, 32, 35, 36, 37, 38, 39, 40, 41	30	1, 6, 7, 8, 9, 10, 11, 12, 14, 16, 17, 19, 20, 22, 24, 26, 27, 28, 29, 30, 32, 34, 35, 36, 37, 38, 39, 40	28
							F6 Risk of insufficient insurance coverage	3, 17, 29	3	1, 3, 17, 29, 39	5
OPERATIONAL							O1 Risk related to project implementation / product and service development (the risk of losses due to inadequate or failed internal processes, human factors, management systems or external events)	2, 3, 4, 6, 7, 9, 14, 17, 18, 19, 20, 21, 23, 28, 29, 32, 33, 35, 38, 39	20	1, 2, 3, 4, 5, 6, 7, 9, 12, 13, 14, 17, 18, 19, 20, 21, 23, 29, 30, 32, 33, 34, 35, 38, 39, 41	26
							O2 Risk related to participation in public tenders (for IT or telecommunication products/services for public administration units)	3, 5, 9, 23, 40	5	3, 19, 40, 41	4

Category					Risk				
STRATEGIC	1, 2, 3, 4, 5, 6, 7, 8, 9, 10, 11, 12, 13, 14, 15, 16, 17, 18, 19, 20, 21, 22, 23, 24, 25, 26, 27, 28, 29, 30, 31, 32, 33, 35, 36, 37, 38, 39, 40, 41	40	98	1, 2, 3, 4, 5, 6, 7, 8, 9, 10, 11, 12, 13, 14, 16, 17, 18, 19, 20, 21, 22, 23, 24, 25, 26, 27, 28, 29, 30, 31, 32, 33, 35, 36, 37, 38, 39, 40, 41	39	95	S1 Risk of failure to achieve strategic objectives/ failure of the strategy (aimed at strengthening the entity's position on the domestic market and expanding into global markets, developing cooperation with current and potential foreign partners, etc.)	1, 4, 7, 9, 12, 18, 22, 24, 25, 29, 30, 35, 36, 38, 39, 40, 41	17	1, 3, 4, 5, 8, 9, 12, 13, 14, 17, 18, 19, 24, 25, 26, 28, 29, 30, 33, 35, 36, 38, 39, 40, 41	25
						S2 Macroeconomic risk (related to the state of the economy in Poland and around the world)	1, 2, 3, 4, 5, 7, 9, 10, 11, 12, 13, 14, 16, 17, 18, 19, 20, 21, 22, 23, 25, 26, 27, 28, 29, 30, 31, 32, 33, 35, 37, 38, 39, 41	34	1, 2, 3, 4, 5, 6, 7, 9, 10, 11, 12, 13, 14, 16, 17, 18, 19, 20, 21, 22, 23, 25, 26, 27, 28, 29, 30, 31, 32, 33, 35, 37, 38, 39, 41	35
						S3 Competition risk (including the risk of losing key customers)	1, 2, 3, 4, 5, 6, 8, 9, 10, 11, 12, 14, 15, 16, 17, 18, 19, 20, 21, 22, 23, 24, 25, 26, 27, 28, 29, 30, 31, 32, 33, 35, 37, 38, 39, 41	36	1, 2, 3, 4, 5, 6, 9, 10, 11, 12, 14, 15, 16, 17, 18, 19, 20, 21, 22, 23, 24, 25, 27, 28, 29, 30, 31, 32, 33, 35, 37, 38, 39, 41	34
						S4 Risk related to COVID-19 pandemic		0	1, 3, 4, 5, 7, 8, 9, 11, 12, 13, 17, 18, 20, 21, 22, 25, 26, 27, 28, 30, 37, 38, 39, 40, 41	25
						S5 Environmental and climate risk		0	3, 8, 9, 22, 25, 26, 38, 39, 40, 41	10
						S6 Risk related to natural disasters, catastrophes or emergencies		0	3, 9, 17, 29, 39, 41	6

(Continued)

Appendix 5.3 (Continued)

Risk category	Entities identifying risks in the particular categories before the pandemic	Total number	Total %	Entities identifying risks in the particular categories during the pandemic	Total number	Total %	Risk factors	Entities identifying a risk factor before the pandemic	Total	Entities identifying a risk factor during the pandemic	Total
BUSINESS	1, 2, 3, 4, 5, 6, 7, 8, 9, 10, 11, 12, 13, 14, 15, 16, 17, 18, 19, 20, 21, 22, 23, 24, 25, 26, 27, 28, 29, 30, 31, 32, 33, 34, 35, 36, 37, 38, 39, 40, 41	41	100	1, 2, 3, 4, 5, 6, 7, 9, 10, 11, 12, 13, 14, 15, 16, 17, 18, 19, 20, 21, 22, 23, 24, 25, 26, 27, 28, 29, 30, 31, 32, 33, 34, 35, 36, 37, 38, 39, 40, 41	40	98	B1 Risk related to the process of winning new contracts and customers, as well as demand for the entities products or services	3, 4, 5, 9, 10, 23, 24, 33, 35	9	1, 3, 4, 5, 6, 7, 9, 10, 11, 12, 13, 14, 16, 23, 24, 25, 26, 27, 28, 29, 31, 35, 38, 39, 40, 41	26
							B2 Financial result risk (the risk of changes in operating costs, insolvency of customer, employment costs) affecting the financial result and business continuity	1, 3, 4, 5, 7, 9, 10, 13, 19, 26, 28, 29, 31, 32, 33, 34, 35, 39, 40, 41	20	1, 2, 3, 4, 5, 9, 10, 11, 12, 13, 14, 17, 18, 19, 20, 24, 25, 26, 27, 28, 29, 30, 31, 32, 33, 34, 35, 37, 38, 39, 40, 41	32		
							B3 Customer concentration risk and risk of dependence on major customers or suppliers	1, 2, 3, 4, 9, 11, 13, 15, 18, 19, 20, 21, 28, 29, 35, 38	16	1, 2, 3, 4, 9, 11, 12, 13, 15, 17, 18, 19, 20, 21, 28, 29, 30, 35, 38	19		
							B4 Risk related to the situation of the sector (including technological changes, development of new technologies, implementation of new products, seasonality of sales)	1, 3, 4, 5, 6, 7, 8, 9, 10, 12, 13, 14, 15, 16, 17, 18, 19, 20, 22, 23, 24, 25, 27, 28, 29, 30, 31, 32, 35, 36, 37, 38, 39, 40, 41	35	1, 3, 5, 6, 10, 11, 12, 13, 14, 15, 16, 17, 18, 19, 21, 22, 24, 25, 26, 27, 28, 29, 30, 32, 35, 36, 37, 38, 39, 40, 41	31		
							B5 Bankruptcy risk		0	26, 38	2		
							B6 Risk of changes in customers' behaviours		0	4, 6, 9, 11, 12, 13, 19, 20, 21, 25, 26, 30, 31, 38, 39, 40, 41	17		

Category	Risk									
REPUTATIONAL	REP1 Reputational risk (the risk to revenue arising from the negative perception of the entity by its customers, counterparties, shareholders, investors, potential business partners)	27	11	2, 3, 4, 9, 11, 17, 19, 35, 38, 39, 41	22	9	2, 3, 4, 9, 11, 19, 35, 38, 39	9 / 2, 3, 4, 9, 11, 19, 35, 38, 39	11 / 2, 3, 4, 9, 11, 17, 19, 35, 38, 39, 41	
REGULATORY	REG1 Non-compliance risk (the risk related to the interpretation, application and changes in legislation, including tax legislation)	85	35	1, 2, 3, 4, 7, 8, 9, 10, 11, 12, 13, 15, 16, 17, 18, 19, 20, 22, 24, 25, 26, 27, 28, 29, 30, 31, 32, 33, 34, 35, 37, 38, 39, 40, 41	85	35	1, 2, 3, 4, 7, 8, 9, 10, 11, 12, 13, 15, 16, 17, 18, 19, 20, 22, 24, 25, 26, 27, 28, 29, 30, 31, 32, 33, 34, 35, 37, 38, 39, 40, 41	33 / 1, 2, 3, 4, 7, 9, 10, 11, 12, 13, 15, 16, 17, 18, 19, 20, 22, 24, 25, 26, 27, 28, 29, 30, 31, 32, 33, 34, 35, 38, 39, 40, 41	33 / 1, 2, 3, 4, 7, 8, 9, 10, 11, 12, 13, 15, 16, 17, 18, 19, 20, 22, 24, 25, 26, 27, 28, 29, 30, 31, 32, 34, 35, 38, 39, 40, 41	
	REG2 Legal risk (the risk of incurring losses due to unfavourable formation of legal relations, unfavourable decisions of courts or other authorities in disputes with other entities, the risk of damages and the risk of infringement of other persons' copyrights or intellectual property rights)							21 / 1, 3, 4, 7, 9, 10, 11, 13, 26, 27, 28, 30, 31, 32, 33, 35, 37, 38, 39, 40, 41	24 / 1, 3, 4, 7, 8, 9, 10, 11, 17, 25, 26, 27, 28, 29, 30, 31, 32, 33, 35, 37, 38, 39, 40, 41	
	REG3 Risk related to licence agreements and concessions							16 / 1, 2, 3, 4, 7, 8, 9, 11, 13, 17, 25, 26, 28, 33, 38, 39	7 / 1, 2, 3, 9, 11, 26, 33	

(Continued)

Appendix 5.3 (Continued)

Risk category	Entities identifying risks in the particular categories before the pandemic	Total number	%	Entities identifying risks in the particular categories during the pandemic	Total number	%	Risk factors	Entities identifying a risk factor before the pandemic	Total	Entities identifying a risk factor during the pandemic	Total
TECHNOLOGICAL	1, 2, 3, 4, 9, 10, 11, 12, 13, 14, 16, 17, 18, 19, 20, 21, 24, 25, 27, 28, 29, 30, 31, 33, 35, 38, 39, 40, 41	29	71	1, 2, 3, 4, 5, 8, 9, 10, 11, 13, 14, 16, 17, 19, 20, 22, 23, 24, 25, 26, 27, 28, 29, 30, 31, 33, 35, 38, 39, 40, 41	31	76	T1 IT supplier and subcontractor risk (related to external suppliers of specialized IT hardware, software and solutions, including the risk of supply chains)	1, 2, 4, 9, 12, 13, 14, 17, 18, 19, 20, 21, 24, 25, 28, 29, 30, 35, 39, 40	20	1, 4, 5, 8, 13, 14, 22, 23, 24, 33, 35, 38, 39, 40, 41	15
							T2 Information systems security risk (the risk of losing personal data, customer information, including the cybercrime risk)	1, 3, 9, 10, 11, 16, 17, 19, 25, 27, 29, 31, 35, 38, 40, 41	16	1, 2, 3, 9, 10, 11, 16, 17, 19, 23, 25, 27, 28, 29, 31, 35, 38, 39, 40, 41	20
							T3 ICT infrastructure failure risk (the risk related to the failure of IT equipment and systems)	1, 3, 9, 10, 11, 17, 25, 29, 30, 31, 33, 35, 38, 39, 40, 41	16	1, 3, 9, 10, 11, 17, 25, 29, 31, 33, 35, 38, 39, 40, 41	15
							T4 Risk related to digitization and continuous technological development		0	1, 2, 3, 4, 9, 11, 19, 20, 23, 26, 28, 29, 30, 31, 38, 39, 40, 41	18

Category	List	n	List	n	n	Risk	n	List	n	List	n
PERSONNEL	1, 2, 3, 4, 5, 6, 7, 8, 9, 10, 12, 13, 15, 16, 17, 18, 19, 20, 21, 22, 23, 25, 26, 28, 30, 31, 33, 35, 36, 37, 38, 39, 40, 41	34	1, 2, 3, 4, 5, 6, 7, 8, 9, 10, 11, 12, 13, 15, 16, 17, 18, 19, 20, 21, 22, 23, 25, 26, 27, 28, 30, 31, 33, 35, 36, 38, 39, 40, 41	83	35	P1 Ethical risk (the risk of unethical actions on the part of employees or third parties; the risk of market abuse, including corruption, illegal copying of innovative solutions)	85	3, 9, 10, 17, 39, 41	6	3, 8, 9, 10, 11, 17, 26, 27, 31, 33, 39, 40, 41	13
						P2 Personnel risk (the risk related to recruitment, availability and professional qualifications of employees, their turnover, adaptability to the work environment, work culture, absenteeism)		1, 2, 3, 4, 5, 6, 7, 8, 9, 10, 12, 13, 15, 16, 17, 18, 19, 20, 21, 22, 23, 25, 26, 28, 30, 31, 33, 35, 36, 37, 38, 39, 40, 41	34	1, 2, 3, 4, 5, 6, 7, 8, 9, 10, 11, 12, 13, 15, 16, 17, 18, 19, 20, 21, 22, 23, 25, 26, 27, 28, 30, 31, 33, 35, 36, 38, 39, 40, 41	35
						P3 Social risk			0	8, 26, 38, 40, 41	5
INVESTMENT	1, 2, 3, 4, 9, 10, 13, 15, 17, 18, 22, 25, 28, 30, 32, 33, 35, 36, 37, 38, 40	21	1, 2, 3, 4, 9, 10, 11, 13, 15, 16, 17, 18, 22, 26, 27, 28, 30, 32, 33, 35, 36, 37, 38, 39, 40	51	25	IN 1 Capital market business cycle risk (the risk of unexpected adverse changes in the value of capital invested in stocks or shares; the risk of issuing the entity's own securities, the risk of transactions between related parties or the risk arising from adverse changes in the shareholding structure)	61	1, 2, 3, 4, 9, 10, 13, 15, 17, 18, 22, 25, 28, 30, 32, 33, 35, 36, 37, 38, 40	21	1, 2, 3, 4, 9, 10, 11, 13, 15, 16, 17, 18, 22, 26, 27, 28, 30, 32, 33, 35, 36, 37, 38, 39, 40	25

Source: The authors' own work.

6 Risk mitigation actions employed by the analysed enterprises representing the financial, construction and IT sectors implemented during the course of the COVID-19 pandemic

Based on the analysis of the source material, we developed a catalogue of actions that the examined enterprises representing the three selected sectors implemented against particular risks during the pandemic (Figure 6.1).

6.1 Strategic changes

In response to the COVID-19 pandemic, the enterprises participating in the research had to implement changes very quickly, not only on an ongoing operational level, but also strategically. The effects of this action very often included a thorough re-modelling of the principles of previous strategies, and sometimes the construction of a completely new strategy to ensure survival during a long-term crisis. The overriding objective of the strategic changes in the examined companies was to ensure the stability of growth despite obstacles and inconveniences in the conduct of business resulting from pandemic-triggered changes. Due to the drastic change in the environment, the companies revised their previous strategic plans, often postponing previously planned projects and focusing mainly on developing and implementing recovery plans for the period after the crisis, which hit the three sectors with different degrees of force.

6.2 Changes in business models

The pandemic also forced the companies under examination to make changes to their business models, often necessitating the implementation of completely new models, due to the inadequacy of the previous ones under the conditions of the pandemic crisis. Even if the previous business model could, to some extent, be applied in response to the crisis, it had to be reorganized and flexibly adapted to the changed conditions. New business models built during the pandemic were also often associated with new investments to ensure business

DOI: 10.4324/9781003514534-6

Figure 6.1 Actions aimed at mitigating risks implemented by the examined enterprises
during the pandemic

Source: The authors' own work.

continuity despite mounting problems with demand, organization, operations,
etc. The consequences of the pandemic also forced the examined enterprises
to restructure their operations, including financial ones.

6.3   Operational changes

In terms of the intensity of the implemented risk mitigation actions, operational
changes predominated among the enterprises participating in the research project. They mainly focused on streamlining and increasing process flexibility,
which was manifested, for example, in measures such as diversification of

activities, suppliers and sales directions or flexible adjustment of resources. Process flexibility was also intensified through the implementation of new ERP systems, already adapted to new pandemic conditions. In the selected enterprises, operational changes were also visible in the form of implemented optimization measures, e.g. increased expenditures on Business Process Management or the use of business analysis tools to a much greater extent than before. In addition, there was a change in the time horizon of contracts, i.e. the enterprises started to opt for long-term contracts to support their operational stability. A strongly outlined area of operational changes during the pandemic was also that of work organization and working conditions, in particular with respect to changes to the work model, reorganization of the work system, optimization of work, procedural simplifications forced by the pandemic, as well as dynamic information and education activities directed at employees in connection with the pandemic.

6.4   Digital transformation

The pandemic strongly pushed the enterprises representing the three selected sectors towards digital transformation. In some companies, related changes were being implemented gradually, while in others, they had the form of a one-off, short and comprehensive process. The main area of the observed transformation was the digitization of processes through the implementation of new technological solutions, automation, digitization of sales and business models, remote access to products and processes, as well as remote customer service. The companies made also extensive use of cloud solutions and implemented electronic workflow systems. In the financial sector, moreover, the expansion of electronic and mobile banking, as well as the development of beyond banking systems were observed. All changes outlined above often resulted in the development of digital transformation strategies in the examined companies. Their implementation required capital expenditure on IT, especially modern infrastructure, fraud detection and cyber security tools, as well as the development of IT systems. Additionally, during the pandemic, the companies started to use artificial intelligence and tools such as liveChat, ChatBot, KnowledgeBase, HelpDesk, Work from Anywhere, PerfectBot much more frequently than before.

6.5   Changes in market relations

Mitigating actions against risks could also be seen in the examined companies in terms of changes in market relations. The first group of activities in this area were customer-related adjustments, in particular: identifying their needs, taking into account changes in customers' preferences, modifying previously developed customer behaviour models, as well as personalizing products and services, most often by way of flexible modifications of the offer. Also, a large number of the examined enterprises either implemented or improved their Efficient Consumer Response (ECR) systems during the pandemic. In addition, the pandemic forced changes in participation in supply chains, particularly evident in the examined construction sector. The companies responded to these changes by introducing shifts to their supply chains, using reserve inventories, implementing intensive logistical changes, as well as amending their existing contracts, for example by extending delivery deadlines. Changes in pricing policies applied by the examined companies also became extremely important in the context of adjustments to market relations, seen in particular in the form of renegotiation of contract terms and prices, modifications in price control and price positioning principles, as well as the building of forecasting models for anticipated price movements.

6.6   Risk management

Of particular relevance to the mitigation actions implemented by the enterprises were those applied directly to risk management systems. Changes in the examined companies' approach to risk management during the pandemic were clearly visible. They manifested themselves, for example, in the development and implementation of a risk and safety culture, the use of expert knowledge, ongoing adaptations to the changing risk profile, advanced forecasting, the expansion of insurance packages and the use of agile models. Changes in risk assessment and analysis methodologies, as well as updates to risk parameter catalogues were also evident. Within the range of risk management activities applied by the examined companies during the pandemic, it is also possible to mention mitigation actions derived from the field of business continuity such as scenario analysis, stress testing and Value at Risk calculations. In order to ensure the continuity of their businesses, some enterprises established special purpose organizational units in the form of crisis management teams, special operational committees or COVID-19 rapid response groups.

6.7   Finance management

Risk mitigation actions in response to the pandemic were also used by the examined companies in the area of finance management. Such actions were mainly focused on reducing costs and maintaining liquidity. In order to reduce costs, measures such as expenditure forecasting, optimization and control of cost fluctuations, cost-saving activities as well as reduction or temporary suspension of dividend payments were used. Besides, the companies were adapting their rating and scoring models to market changes related to the pandemic. In order to ensure liquidity in the conditions of the pandemic crisis, the enterprises participating in the research, among other things, implemented specific customer financing and monitoring rules, established additional accounting provisions for risks related to expected losses, adjusted and optimized their credit policies, applied limits and guarantee instruments, shortened receivables turnover cycles and implemented strategies aimed at diversifying revenue sources. Also, during the pandemic a large proportion of the companies used external support tools, such as statutory and non-statutory moratoria, public guarantee schemes, aid packages, and credit instalment payment suspension mechanisms. The intensive use of safe banking products and changes in due diligence rules were noticeable as well.

7 Risk profiling and enterprise resilience

7.1 The impact of risk management on the creation of resilience mechanisms

A company's resilience is defined as its ability to recover to a state that guarantees survival and to acquire skills necessary to operate in disruptive conditions. Resilience is characterized by the following features: (1) it is a non-continuous capability, (2) it emphasizes survival and the ability to adapt to and thrive in a difficult situation and (3) it is multi-level in nature and maintains a relationship with resources, processes and procedures (Xiao & Cao, 2017). Furthermore, building its resilience, an enterprise focuses on the development of its unique capabilities useful in coping with uncertain situations (Ma et al., 2018). It is also worth noting that resilience refers to a systemic category (mainly ecological, economic, social and organizational systems) and denotes the ability to return to normal conditions after a destructive event that alters its state (Morales et al., 2019).

We believe that the definition of resilience should be expanded. Obviously, the question of a business organization's ability to restore its functions after a crisis is an indicator of the level of resilience possessed, but resilience should also have a dimension of preventive measures. This means that companies should constantly prepare for the arrival of hypothetical crises by creating an environment for testing different solutions under simulation conditions. This is only possible through continuous, systematic and constantly updated risk management procedures. Thus, the definition of resilience that we propose indicates that the resilience of an enterprise is its ability to prevent the occurrence of a crisis or to minimize the scale and severity of its negative effects (once the occurrence of a crisis cannot be prevented) while preserving its key functions allowing for the continuation of its operations and ensuring the possibility of further development after the crisis has passed. In other words, we understand resilience through the prism of both preventive measures (before a crisis occurs) and corrective measures (during and after a crisis).

The increasingly chaotic business environment is now indicated as a major source of increasing demand for high levels of business resilience (Kantur &

DOI: 10.4324/9781003514534-7

İşeri-Say, 2015). This is why an in-depth understanding of its role in business management is so important. This understanding of the importance of resilience in the functioning of contemporary enterprises is facilitated by resilience models, such as the compensation model, the provocation model, the protection model or the vulnerability model (Ledesma, 2014). Enterprise resilience is also categorized. Firstly, a distinction is made between hard resilience (understood as the direct strength of a company's structures) and soft resilience (understood as the ability of systems to absorb trouble and recover from negative impacts) (Proag, 2014). Secondly, resilience can also be categorized based on the domains that characterize it. Three complementary domains can be distinguished as a guarantee of an enterprise's stability. These are the behavioural domain, the growth domain and the performance domain (Hillmann & Guenther, 2020). Thirdly, the resilience-building capacity of a company is also categorized. In view of this, the following are distinguished: anticipatory capacity, coping capacity and adaptive capacity (Duchek, 2020).

In summary, enterprise resilience has several important characteristics, which include redundancy, absorbing capability, recovery capability, situation awareness, management of keystone vulnerabilities, adaptive capability, risk intelligence, agility, awareness, preparedness, flexibility, diversity, efficiency, adaptability, cohesion, collaboration, risk management culture, visibility (Erol et al., 2010). However, for an enterprise to be able to develop the aforementioned resilience traits, the shaping of resilience mechanisms should start with the integration of three foundational elements, namely: culture of preparedness, business continuity and disaster resilience (Jedynak & Bąk, 2021).

Enterprise resilience mechanisms are determined to the greatest extent by the effectiveness of the risk management system in place. It can be argued that a risk management system is the basis for building resilience. The greater the commitment and effort that is devoted to updating, intensifying and expanding the risk management system, the more likely it is that the resilience mechanisms implemented will be effective. We were led to this conclusion by the findings of current research, indicating that:

- implemented risk mitigation measures support the achievement of recovery-based resilience and reconfiguration-based resilience (Soufi et al., 2021),
- a risk management system contributes to building strategic resilience (Natale et al., 2022),
- enterprise resilience is firmly rooted in Enterprise Risk Management (ERM) (Louisot, 2015),
- the risk management culture in place has a key impact on the resilience of supply chains (Kumar & Anbanandam, 2019),
- corporate resilience is a key property of risk management, created in response to new and severe crisis events (Dahmen, 2023),
- a sustainability-based risk management system determines flexibility and resilience in decision-making (Settembre-Blundo et al., 2021),

- a key manifestation of corporate resilience is adequate preparation for risks and the prevention of their cascading effects in all operating areas of an enterprise (Herrington, 2023),
- corporate resilience is a top priority in the strategic decision-making process for risk management (FERMA, 2021),
- risk and insurance managers need to be intensively involved in improving resilience levels (FERMA, 2021),
- foresight capabilities (scenarios and stress testing) are key areas for strengthening corporate resilience (FERMA, 2021),
- the risk function and executive teams rather than strategy teams play a role in building resilient enterprises (FERMA, 2021),
- there is an apparent need among companies to improve their risk cultures and integrate resilience more strongly into strategies (FERMA, 2021),
- an enterprise's resilience is a dynamic property that is measured by the stability and sustainability of its value in a changing environment; in turn, this stability and sustainability is dependent on the effectiveness of an enterprise's risk management processes (Sheth & Sinfield, 2023).

7.2 The role of risk profiling in measuring and improving enterprise resilience

Risk profiling correlates very strongly with a company's resilience mechanisms. In essence, it can be said that risk profiling processes, if reliably implemented and updated in line with changes in the environment, pave the way for building and continuously strengthening the level of resilience. The interdependencies between risk profiling and enterprise resilience are presented in detail in Figure 7.1.

Building on the step-by-step risk profiling process we developed in Chapter 3, it can be seen that a company's level of resilience is influenced by the three key stages of risk profiling: (1) planning and building a risk profile, (2) designing and implementing risk mitigation actions, and (3) continually updating the risk profile based on the monitoring of the environment.

The prepared risk profile first of all provides a procedural basis for initiating the process of building an enterprise's resilience and, in particular, creating resilience mechanisms vis-à-vis a possible materialization of key risks, i.e., those that pose the greatest threat to the company and must therefore be addressed with particular care. In addition, the construction of a risk profile makes it possible to tailor preventive actions to the current catalogue of risk factors included in the profile. This can be applied in crisis prevention, i.e., situations in which the occurrence of a crisis can be prevented. Another manifestation of the impact of risk profiling on business resilience is the precise planning of corrective actions. This, in turn, applies in situations where the occurrence of a crisis cannot be prevented, but an enterprise can neutralize or reduce the scale of its negative effects. Business resilience should also be tested regularly. This means that the "tester" of resilience should not only be actual crises, but

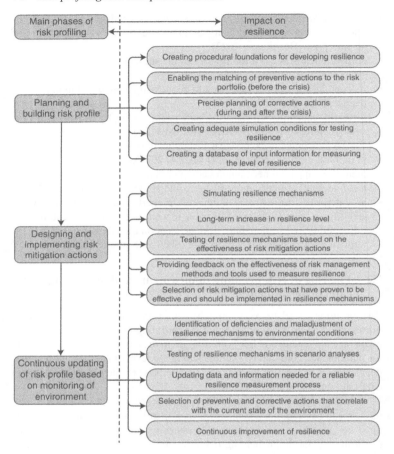

Figure 7.1 Interdependencies between risk profiling and enterprise resilience
Source: The authors' own work.

first and foremost resilience should be checked under conditions realistically simulating crisis situations of various types. Risk profiling creates adequate simulation conditions for resilience to be continually tested against different risk options. Risk profiling processes also play a major role in measuring the levels of resilience. At the stage of building a risk profile, this role manifests itself in the form of creating an input database for the measurement procedures implemented with a view to assessing the current level of resilience.

The stage in risk profiling that comprises the design and implementation of risk mitigation actions also affects resilience, its level and the motivators for strengthening it. Firstly, mitigation actions definitely stimulate the generation of mechanisms enhancing an organization's resilience to specific risk factors. Secondly, a mitigation action plan enables the initiation and implementation of a long-term resilience improvement process. Furthermore, based on the results of evaluating the effectiveness of designed and implemented risk mitigation measures, it is possible to test resilience mechanisms at multiple levels. In addition, feedback on the risk management methods and tools used as part of the designed mitigation actions constitutes key information in resilience measurement processes. Another manifestation of the impact of risk mitigation on resilience is the possibility to select those mitigation actions that have proven to be effective and should be permanently incorporated into an enterprise's core resilience mechanisms.

The next stage of risk profiling, which is the continual updating of the developed profile based on the uninterrupted monitoring of the environment, also plays a role in the processes of building and strengthening resilience. Above all, it enables the identification of weaknesses and maladaptation of resilience mechanisms to current environmental conditions. By recognizing such shortcomings, it is possible to improve resilience mechanisms. Also, updating the risk profile helps to use scenario analyses in testing resilience mechanisms that can be subsequently implemented in the event of different types of potential threats. The updated risk profile should also allow for the renewal of data and information needed for regular and reliable resilience measurement procedures. Additionally, by adjusting changes in the risk profile to changes in the environment, enterprises can selectively choose preventive and corrective measures (targeted at risks and their effects) that correlate with the current state of the environment. The final aspect of the impact of the continuous updating of the risk profile on the resilience of the company is manifested in the possibilities for continuous improvement of resilience, i.e., raising its level and ensuring stronger protection against new or previously known but intensified risks.

7.3   Practical implications of the interdependencies between risk profiling and enterprise resilience

Our empirical research into the risk profiles of the selected enterprises in the financial, construction and IT sectors, as well as changes in their activities caused by the COVID-19 pandemic, has various practical implications. The results of our research and observations of the business environment before, during and after the pandemic crisis allowed us to identify a number of interdependencies between risk profiling and enterprise resilience. The main ones are the following:

- Risk prioritization, which is one of the main steps in the risk profiling process, makes it possible to identify major risks: (1) faced by a given enterprise (relating to its individual circumstances), (2) occurring at a specific time and situation in which an enterprise finds itself (resulting from the macroeconomic situation) and (3) typical of the sector in which an enterprise operates. With such a diagnosis, an enterprise has full knowledge of which risks need to be managed with the utmost care at a particular time, as inadequate responses to the occurrence of priority risks can seriously undermine its position. Thus, prioritization of risks supports the processes of building and shaping resilience to those risks that are critical at any given time.

- Continuous monitoring of the environment with a view to ensuring that risk profile data are up to date helps, firstly, to create resilience mechanisms adapted to changes in the environment and, secondly, makes resilience measurement procedures more realistic, which means that they are always performed on the basis of the current state of an enterprise's risk management system.

- The knowledge, skills and resources used to build a risk profile can and should be used to shape and strengthen resilience to crises. With regard to this issue, we see an intensive feedback loop between data and information included in a risk profile and used to develop resilience mechanisms and, conversely, between information on the effectiveness or ineffectiveness of resilience mechanisms introduced into a risk profile for the purpose of its updating and improvement.

- Assessments of the probability of occurrence and the impact of particular identified risk factors on an enterprise's operations can be successfully used in procedures aimed at measuring its resilience to such risk factors.

- The cyclically conducted risk profiling process makes it possible to very quickly capture changes in companies' exposure to different types of risks, both under normal operating conditions and during crises. As a result, companies are made aware almost immediately of changes in the landscape of risks surrounding them and can very effectively and dynamically adapt their risk management approaches to such identified changes. This, in turn, translates naturally into strengthening their resilience, in both the preventive and corrective dimensions.

- Risk profiling processes make it possible to very quickly diagnose new risks which arise in crisis situations and which were included in a given enterprise's risk portfolio prior to their occurrence. New, previously unknown risks pose the greatest threat to businesses because relevant defence mechanisms against them have not been developed yet. Rapidly identified and communicated new risks appear to be an indicator of the creation of new resilience mechanisms in the event of the emergence of such new risks.

- Sector-specific risk profiles make it possible for enterprises representing individual sectors, firstly, to become aware of the current risks in their immediate environment (especially when enterprises do not individually carry out risk profiling processes) and, secondly, to compare individual sectors in terms of their security or exposure to different types of risks. Such information can be extremely useful to, for example, company shareholders, current and potential investors, customers, business partners, members of a supply chain or other stakeholder groups. From a macroeconomic perspective, sector-specific risk profiles are also relevant for a country's economy. By diagnosing the risk landscape of each sector, government authorities can, for example, decide on forms of support for the sectors affected at a given point in time, or use such information as support in analysing changes in macroeconomic indexes. Such measures can make a visible contribution to increasing the resilience of national economies to crises.

- The risk mitigation process, which is a mandatory step in risk profiling, can in principle be viewed by enterprises as a yardstick for assessing the level of resilience. This is because properly designed and successfully implemented risk mitigation actions determine whether an enterprise overcomes a crisis situation and maximally neutralizes the negative effects of the risks that triggered the crisis. Thus, the effectiveness of mitigation actions can be considered as a determinant of the effectiveness of resilience mechanisms.

- Risk mitigation actions can also be part of sector-specific benchmarking. For example, industry leaders who manage to develop effective ways of mitigating risks in crisis situations can be role models for smaller and less experienced sector representatives. This approach can indeed have a positive impact on the level of a given sector's resilience.

- Risk mitigation actions should be developed, tested and implemented both under normal operating conditions and in crisis situations. Mitigation actions tested under simulated conditions in the event of various hypothetical threats are much more effective in confrontation with a real crisis situation and more effectively increase a company's level of resilience than actions taken on an ad hoc basis already during a crisis.

- Thanks to the continuous monitoring of data and information needed to update their profiles, enterprises involved in risk profiling are characterized by a higher level of resilience to crises, which manifests itself mainly in greater effectiveness in addressing new or intensified risks, the adequacy of implemented mitigating measures, as well as the dynamism and extent of preventive defence mechanisms.

Bibliography

Dahmen, P. (2023). Organizational Resilience as a Key Property of Enterprise Risk Management in Response to Novel and Severe Crisis Events. Risk Management and Insurance Review, 26(2), 203–345. DOI: 10.1111/rmir.12245

Duchek, S. (2020). Organizational Resilience: a Capability-Based Conceptualization. Business Research, 13, 215–246. doi: 10.1007/s40685-019-0085-7

Erol, O., Sauser, B. J., Mansouri, M. (2010). A Framework for Investigation into Extended Enterprise Resilience. Enterprise Information Systems, 4(2), 111–136.

FERMA (2021). The role of risk management in corporate resilience. Survey Report. https://www.ferma.eu/app/uploads/2021/09/FERMA-Resilience-Report-fina_CL_ 27.09.pdf (Access: 1.03.2024).

Herrington, M. (2023). Investing in Your Company's Physical Risk Resilience. Harvard Business Review, https://hbr.org/2023/08/investing-in-your-companys-physical-risk-resilience (Access: 1.03.2024).

Hillmann, J., Guenther, E. (2020). Organizational Resilience: A Valuable Construct for Management Research? International Journal of Management Reviews, 23(1), 7–44. DOI: 10.1111/ijmr.12239

Jedynak, P., Bąk, S. (2021). Risk Management in Crisis: Winners and Losers during the COVID-19 Pandemic, London, New York: Routledge. DOI: 10.4324/9781003131366

Kantur, D., İşeri-Say, A. (2015). Organizational Resilience: A Conceptual Integrative Framework. Journal of Management & Organization, 18(6), 762–773. DOI: 10.5172/jmo.2012.18.6.762

Kumar, S., Anbanandam, R. (2019). Impact of Risk Management Culture on Supply Chain Resilience: An Empirical Study from Indian Manufacturing Industry. Proceedings of the Institution of Mechanical Engineers Part O Journal of Risk and Reliability, 234(3). DOI: 10.1177/1748006X19886718

Ledesma, J. (2014). Conceptual Frameworks and Research Models on Resilience in Leadership. SAGE Open, 4(3), 1–8. DOI: 10.1177/2158244014545464

Louisot, J.-P. (2015). Risk and/or Resilience Management. Risk Governance and Control Financial Markets & Institutions, 5(2), 84–91. DOI: 10.22495/rgcv5i2c1art2

Ma, Z., Xiao, L., Yin, J. (2018). Toward a Dynamic Model of Organizational Resilience. Nankai Business Review International, 9(3), 246–263. DOI: 10.1108/NBRI-07-2017-0041

Morales, S. N., Martínez, L. R., Gómez, J. A. H., López, R. R., Torres-Argüelles, V. (2019). Predictors of Organizational Resilience by Factorial Analysis. International Journal of Engineering Business Management, 11, 1–13. DOI: 10.1177/1847979019837046

Natale, A., Poppensieker, T., Thun, M. (2022). From risk management to strategic resilience. McKinesy, https://www.mckinsey.com/capabilities/risk-and-resilience/our-insights/from-risk-management-to-strategic-resilience (Access: 1.03.2024).

Proag, V. (2014). The Concept of Vulnerability and Resilience. Procedia Economics and Finance, 18, 369–376. DOI: 10.1016/S2212-5671(14)00952-6

Settembre-Blundo, D., González-Sánchez, R., Medina-Salgado, S., García-Muiña, F. E. (2021). Flexibility and Resilience in Corporate Decision Making: A New Sustainability-Based Risk Management System in Uncertain Times. Global Journal of Flexible Systems Management, 22, 107–132. DOI: 10.1007/s40171-021-00277-7

Sheth, A., Sinfield, J. V. (2023). Risk Intelligence and the Resilient Company. MIT Sloan Management Review, https://sloanreview.mit.edu/article/risk-intelligence-and-the-resilient-company/ (Access: 1.03.2024).

Soufi, H. R., Esfahanipour, A., Shirazi, M. A. (2021). Risk Reduction through Enhancing Risk Management by Resilience. International Journal of Disaster Risk Reduction, 64, 102497. DOI: 10.1016/j.ijdrr.2021.102497

Xiao, L., Cao, H. (2017). Organizational Resilience: The Theoretical Model and Research Implication. ITM Web of Conferences, 12(18), 04021. DOI: 10.1051/itmconf/20171204021

Conclusions

Compared to previous studies on the risks faced by enterprises during the COVID-19 pandemic (e.g. Donthu & Gustafsson, 2020; Grondys et al., 2021; Kaushal & Srivastava, 2021; Saragih et al., 2021; Drydakis, 2022; Kaya, 2022), our research and its findings constitute a much stronger contribution to the understanding of the actual risks faced by business organizations during the pandemic crisis. Firstly, thanks to the fact that our research followed a set structure in parallel for the two periods (before and during the pandemic), we were able to identify entirely new risks that had only emerged during the pandemic and had not previously been included in the risk profiles of the examined enterprises. This allowed us to create a catalogue of risks that are a direct consequence of the pandemic, which has important implications for the management of companies in the post-pandemic period and for building their resilience to subsequent crises. Secondly, by conducting two analogous studies, we were able to verify the level of the pandemic-triggered change in the selected enterprises' exposure to the risks that had already been included in their risk profiles before the pandemic. This outcome is also important for the business world, as the precise determination of the intensity of changes in the area of individual risks in a crisis situation provides managers with knowledge of which particular risks require more intensive preventive measures and helps them to plan long-term resilience strategies.

Thanks to the results of the second part of our research, i.e., the identification of mitigating actions implemented by the examined companies against risks during the pandemic, we were able to reproduce specific instrumentation of mitigating actions adequate for use in crisis situations such as the COVID-19 pandemic. Compared to other studies in this area (cf. 'Thürmer et al., 2020; Bai et al., 2021; Belas et al., 2021; Engidaw, 2022; Ma'ady et al., 2022; Louaas & Picard, 2023; Reineholm et al., 2023), which identified fragmentary preventive actions applied during the pandemic, the results of our study constitute a comprehensive overview of the mitigating actions applied by the examined companies at the time. Furthermore, due to the fact that the research covered enterprises representing three very diverse business sectors, the obtained results bear the hallmark of universality.

DOI: 10.4324/9781003514534-8

Our inter-sectoral analyses carried out on the basis of the research results and indicating what changes took place in the area of risks and how companies in the respective sectors were able to deal with these risks can be extremely useful to various stakeholder groups, for example counterparties, business partners, as well as current and potential investors. This is because we constructed risk profiles of enterprises representing the financial, construction and IT sectors, diagnosed the changes that had occurred in their respective operational areas as a result of the pandemic and identified in detail the measures implemented in response to new or changed risks. This is therefore useful information for assessing the examined companies' resilience to and preparedness for crisis situations.

In the conditions of a crisis, the overriding objective should be to ensure business continuity (Assibi, 2022) and, thanks to the results of our research, it is possible to assess in detail how actions aimed at mitigating particular risks and, in principle, ensuring business continuity are aligned with a given enterprise's current risk profile. Thus, the final conclusion that could be drawn from our work is that a company's risk profile must be continuously updated, even in non-crisis conditions, because only prompt and adequate mitigating actions implemented in response to a crisis on the basis of an updated risk profile offer a chance of success in overcoming difficulties.

We believe that our original risk profiling process diagram and the accompanying guidelines can help enterprises to better manage not only risks specified in their risk profiles, but also their resilience to crises by strengthening their resilience mechanisms and continuously updating inputs to the profiling process in both crisis and safe business conditions.

Our research contributes to the development of theoretical and managerial knowledge in several ways. Firstly, on the basis of our research on risk management processes, we defined an enterprise's risk profile. By conceptualizing this notion, it will be possible to implement a new approach to risk management in business organizations that is more advanced and better adapted to the current market realities. By identifying and establishing an enterprise's risk profile, it is possible to identify and prioritize existing threats, as well as to plan, build and improve risk management systems oriented towards a specific risk profile. Thus, the identification of each enterprise's risk profile (and its continuous updating) appears to be one of the most important determinants of the effectiveness of risk management systems.

The second element of the contribution of our research to the development of management sciences is providing empirical evidence on how a crisis of an unpredictable nature and unprecedented course, such as the COVID-19 pandemic, affect changes in the risk profiles of enterprises representing the three selected important sectors of the economy. Indeed, the realities of a pandemic generate new challenges for every organization's risk management practices.

The third important outcome of the research presented in this book is the identification of mitigating actions taken by the examined enterprises against the risk factors included in their respective risk profiles during the pandemic. The study of this aspect not only is important in view of achieving the established diagnostic objectives, but also examines how enterprises dealt with the risks whose occurrence they had not been able to foresee and, consequently, were not able to counteract by means of any previously developed mitigating actions. It is therefore an important element in testing the effectiveness of not only the enterprises' existing risk management systems, but also their cultures of preparedness, business continuity and disaster resilience, which are the three domains of a model for implementing resilience mechanisms in business organizations (Jedynak & Bąk, 2021).

The fourth major achievement of our analyses has been the demonstration of processual interdependencies between risk profiling and the building or strengthening of resilience. We have shown that structured, logical, continuous and updated risk profiling procedures contribute, firstly, to building an enterprise's resilience and, secondly, to strengthening it on an ongoing basis. We have been able to do this by identifying the impact of risk management on the creation of resilience mechanisms and by demonstrating the role that risk profiling processes play in measuring and improving resilience. The achievement of this objective has also been facilitated by the formulation of practical implications resulting from our research.

Also, our research has led us to a conclusion indicating that risk profiling (and particularly the preparation, quality, reliability, continuity and updating of this process) is a very important factor influencing enterprise resilience.

Bibliography

Assibi, A. T. (2022). The Role of Enterprise Risk Management in Business Continuity and Resiliency in the Post-COVID-19 Period. Open Access Library Journal, 9(6), 1–19. DOI: 10.4236/oalib.1108642

Bai, C., Quayson, M., Sarkis, J. (2021). COVID-19 Pandemic Digitization Lessons for Sustainable Development of Micro-and Small- Enterprises. Sustainable Production and Consumption, 27, 1989–2001. DOI: 10.1016/j.spc.2021.04.035

Belas, J., Gavurova, B., Dvorsky, J., Cepel, M., Durana, P. (2021). The Impact of the COVID-19 Pandemic on Selected Areas of a Management System in SMEs. Economic Research-Ekonomska Istraživanja, 35(1), 3757–3777. DOI: 10.1080/1331677X.2021.2004187

Donthu, N., Gustafsson, A. (2020). Effects of COVID-19 on Business and Research. Journal of Business Research, 117, 284–289. DOI: 10.1016/j.jbusres.2020.06.008

Drydakis, N. (2022). Artificial Intelligence and Reduced SMEs' Business Risks. A Dynamic Capabilities Analysis During the COVID-19 Pandemic. Information Systems Frontiers, 24, 1223–1247. DOI: 10.1007/s10796-022-10249-6

Engidaw, A. E. (2022). Small Businesses and Their Challenges During COVID-19 Pandemic in Developing Countries: in the Case of Ethiopia. Journal of Innovation and Entrepreneurship, 11(1), 1–14. DOI: 10.1186/s13731-021-00191-3

Grondys, K., Ślusarczyk, O., Hussain, H. I., Androniceanu, A. (2021). Risk Assessment of the SME Sector Operations During the COVID-19 Pandemic. International

Journal of Environmental Research and Public Health, 18(8), 4183. DOI: 10.3390/ijerph18084183

Jedynak, P., Bąk, S. (2021). Risk Management in Crisis: Winners and Losers During the COVID-19 Pandemic, London, New York: Routledge. DOI: 10.4324/9781003131366

Kaushal, V., Srivastava, S. (2021). Hospitality and Tourism Industry Amid COVID-19 Pandemic: Perspectives on Challenges and Learnings from India. International Journal of Hospitality Management, 92, 1–9. DOI: 10.1016/j.ijhm.2020.102707

Kaya, O. (2022). Determinants and Consequences of SME Insolvency Risk during the Pandemic. Economic Modelling, 115, 105958. DOI: 10.1016/j.econmod.2022.105958

Louaas, A., Picard, P. (2023). A Pandemic Business Interruption Insurance. The Geneva Risk and Insurance Review, 48, 1–30. DOI: 10.1057/s10713-023-00080-7

Ma'ady, M. N. P., Vanany, I., Mardhiana, H., Albana, A. S. (2022). The Important of Supply Chain Resilience During Covid-19 Pandemic For Enterprise Risk Management: A Systematic Literature Review. Proceedings of the 1st International Conference on Contemporary Risk Studies, ICONIC-RS 2022, 31 March-1 April 2022, South Jakarta, DKI Jakarta, Indonesia. https://eudl.eu/doi/10.4108/eai.31-3-2022.2320664 (Access: 13.04.2023).

Reineholm, C., Ståhl, C., Lundqvist, D. (2023). Bringing Risk Back in: managers' Prioritization of the Work Environment During the Pandemic. International Journal of Workplace Health Management, 16(1), 4–19. DOI: 10.1108/IJWHM-03-2022-0041

Saragih, S., Setiawan, S., Markus, T., Rhian, P. (2021). Benefits and Challenges of Telework During The Covid-19 Pandemic. International Journal of Business Studies, 14(2), 129–136. DOI: 10.21632/irjbs.14.2.129-135

Thürmer, J. L., Wieber, F., Gollwitzer, P. M. (2020). Management in Times of Crisis: Can Collective Plans Prepare Teams to Make and Implement Good Decisions? Management Decision, 58(10), 2155–2176. DOI: 10.1108/MD-08-2020-1088

Index

Note: Figures are indicated by *italics*. Tables are indicated by **bold**.

artificial intelligence 9, 72

business continuity 1, 8–9, 19, 28, 45,
  73, 76, 84–5
business continuity management 2, 8, 19
Business Continuity Plan *5*
business model 7, 10, 37–8, 70–2
business resilience 31, 75, 77
business risk 15, 18, *37–9*, 41, *43–4*, *46*

change management 7
climate risk 38, 44, **51**, **58**, **65**
compliance *2*, 9, 29, **51**, **53–4**, **61**, **67**
contingency plan 29, 38, **51**
corporate culture 18
corporate management system 1–2
credit risk 9, 38, **57**, **64**
crisis prevention *5*, 8, 77
crisis-related changes 17
culture of preparedness *5*, 18, 76
cyber threats 30

decision-making process 29, 77
digital transformation 19, 39, 45, **53**,
  71–2
Disaster Recovery Plan *5*
disaster resilience 76, 85
Disaster Management Cycle 17

Early Warning System *5*
economic risk 10
Enterprise Management System *1–2*
Enterprise Risk Management (ERM) 1,
  3, 19, 76
enterprise strategy *2*

finance management *71*, 73
financial risk 9, 18, 23, 36–*7*, *39*, 41,
  43, *46*

hybrid working 18

insurance risk **57**
investment risk *37*, *39*, *43*, *46*

leadership 19
Lean Management 7
legal risk 9, 36, 40, **53**, **61**, **67**
liquidity risk **49**, **57**, **63**

macroeconomic conditions 36, **51**
macroeconomic risk 40, **59**, **65**
market relations 72–3,
mitigation strategies 14–15,

natural disaster 44, **58**, **65**

operational changes *71–2*
operational risk 9, *37*, *39*, 41–*3*, *46–7*,
  52, **58**
operations management *2*
organizational culture *5*, 6, 9

personnel risk 9, *37–9*, 42–*6*, **54**, **62**, **69**
proactive risk management 29
project management 15, 30

risk appetite 23
regulatory risk *37*, *39*, *43*, *46*
reputational risk *37*, *39*, *43*, *46–7*, **52**,
  61, **67**

resilience management 18
risk intelligence 76
risk management culture 76
risk management teams 17
risk mitigation process 17, 81
risk mitigation strategies 14–17
risk prioritization 79

scenario analyses 79
skills 27, 75, 80

standardized risk management 4
strategic changes *70–1*
strategic management 1, *2*, 7
strategic resilience 76
strategic risk management 4

technological risk 9, 15, 36–*7*, *39*, *43*,
    45–7

Warsaw Stock Exchange 32